D1326415

VALUE

Value

What Money Can't Buy

A Handbook for Practical Hedonism

Stephen Bayley

CONSTABLE

CONSTABLE

First published in Great Britain in 2021 by Constable

1 3 5 7 9 10 8 6 4 2

Extract of 'Good-bye to the Mezzogiorno', *Collected Poems*, W.H. Auden, reproduced with permission of Curtis Brown. (p106)

A CIP catalogue record for this book
is available from the British Library.

ISBN: 978-1-47213-491-2 (hardback)

Typeset in Bembo by SX Composing DTP, Rayleigh, Essex
Printed and bound in Great Britain by Clays Ltd, Elcograf, S.p.A.

Papers used by Constable are from well-managed forests
and other responsible sources.

MIX
Paper from
responsible sources
FSC® C104740

Constable
An imprint of
Little, Brown Book Group
Carmelite House
50 Victoria Embankment
London EC4Y 0DZ

An Hachette UK Company
www.hachette.co.uk

www.littlebrown.co.uk

To Flo, as ever. But also Bruno, Coco, Cass, Ellis, Ollie and Pintxo.

CONTENTS

'Why is it so difficult to assemble those things that really matter and to dwell among them only? I am referring to certain landscapes, persons, beasts, books, rooms, meteorological conditions, fruits.'

James Salter

'Our business here is the conscientious, continuous, resolute distinction of quality from mediocrity.'

Alfred H. Barr on the founding of the Museum of Modern Art, New York

'Those whom the gods love do not die young; they live to be old, remaining quick to learn and feel.'

Raymond Mortimer on Bernard Berenson

Francis Galton, Charles Darwin's cousin and an unfettered polymath, eugenicist, traveller and adventurer, felt there was a right and a wrong way to roll up your shirt sleeves. (He also recommended gunpowder in warm water as a reliable emetic. He was right about the shirt sleeves, but probably wrong about the gunpowder.)

Q. What's more valuable, a fifty-pound sack of potatoes or a one-ounce tin of caviar?

A. The potatoes, obviously. They have far more creative potential and require some satisfying technique to make delicious. You only need to open the tin of caviar. Yet the small amount of caviar would, unquestionably, cause a short moment of intense pleasure.

But a potato is more challenging. The caviar cannot be improved. But the potato can. In an almost infinite number of ways.

(However, in an *ideal* world you would have *both*, since there is almost nothing quite so good as a simple baked potato with a small splash of sour cream and a sprinkle of Caspian sturgeon's eggs.)

Heathrow, 5 February 2020

I have flown more than most. One year, long ago, an average of eight hours a week for a year. And I certainly do not repudiate air travel.

At its best, flying is a supreme reconciliation of technology, consumerism and wine-tasting with the occasional mystical insight . . . the latter caused, perhaps, by Peruvian Chardonnay and oxygen deprivation as much as spiritual elevation.

Surely, only the dullest person would not be moved by the circumstances of sitting five miles high, above the clouds, skirmishing on the edge of space. The world and its cares seem happily distant with a glass of airline wine to hand and a view to rival the gods'.

And arrival is always a thrill, and a relief, wherever it is. But especially in one of those places – Nice or Lisbon, say – when they open the plane door and an emollient wave of warm, damp air (lightly tinged by the pungent smell of avgas) says you are a long way from home. The sight of a palm tree or oleander is also very welcome.

I don't claim even amateur clairvoyance, let alone well-developed second sight, but on this bright February morning

I was in the BA lounge at Heathrow, and it was just a few days before the Spanish began, perforce, to take the new and invasive virus very seriously. And I was on my way to Barcelona.

Of course, I have always recognised what a shocking indulgence air travel is. But I like indulgences. Still, this day at nine in the morning with a glass of champagne (you have to nag for it, but eventually it will come), I looked across the vast vista of what was long ago Hounslow Heath − where highwaymen once did their business − and found myself thinking 'Whatever is going to become of us?'

All the way to the hazy horizon, the landscape was given to aircraft and the apparatus of flight. Lumbering jets manoeuvred like tranquillised elephants. Service vehicles buzzed around them fussily. I am not going to say 'Dance of Death', because that would be morbidly inappropriate, but it was certainly a slo-mo masque of magnificent futility and shaming absurdity. I became dismayed by what an out-of-control waste-production system flying had become. Expensive. Dirty. Damaging. I asked for another glass of champagne.

Can this weird global conspiracy − so out of the reach of governments − ever be reformed, I wondered. What ends could possibly justify the wanton expense of so many precious and rare resources?

It was only a minor revelation and scarcely an original one. But how little I realised that this would be my last return flight for a long time. I left Spain to return to London a week later, just as the medical news became more sinister than anybody had anticipated.

And air travel would never be the same again. Perhaps nothing would ever be the same again.

Value

The highest forms of enjoyment are free

'There is no wealth, but life.'

John Ruskin, *Unto This Last* (1860)

Let's see what money can't buy.

Whiskery Chinese sages in their streaming wet caves – I am thinking of Ying Chu – knew that the most valuable things in the world are beyond the reach of cash. Literally priceless. Indeed, they are beyond any sort of measurement.

The only things you can measure are banal: you can attach a number to the height of, say, a table. But 'eighty-five centimetres' tells you very little. It only tells you that it is higher than a seventy-centimetre table and lower than one a metre tall. Your measurement will not tell you if it is a beautiful table. Nor an ugly one. And something altogether more mysterious tells you whether it's a table you like or dislike.

That's the uncertainty forever attending any conversation about taste, which is the business of deciding what we like: it's way beyond the reach of science. Meanwhile, nor can love, desire, charm, fantasy and wit be determined in centimetres or kilos . . . nor even in bytes. But they can all be enjoyed without spending much money. **Basically, the highest forms of enjoyment are free. Or, at least, not very expensive.**

'My capital is time, not money' was Marcel Duchamp's withering response to a question about why he spent his last years playing chess instead of realising the cash 'value' of his revolutionary art. Duchamp it was who told us that a porcelain urinal sourced in a plumbers' depot could, viewed correctly and signed by the artist, be seen as 'art' (although some attribute this powerful and disturbing insight to his collaborator, the zany Elsa von Freytag-Loringhoven. Although to give Elsa her due, we need a bigger word than 'zany'.)

But Duchamp always tiptoed along a line between cynical fraud and blinding astonishment. Anyway, while great wealth remains elusive to most of us, time is capital we all possess, although it's a diminishing asset for everyone. And it's every individual's privilege to decide how best to spend it.

© 1963 Julian Wasser

Marcel Duchamp refused to cash in on his revolutionary art and spent the latter part of his life playing chess every single day. In 1963, memorably so with a nude Eve Babitz.

To pursue the image: wisely invested, capital should generate interest. And any investment of time should create value. Not, I mean, in those rare moments of exaltation in the presence of great art, although great art is very strongly recommended, but 60/60/24/7/365 until the Crack of Doom.

There's no good reason why the thrill of art cannot be enjoyed every single day, whether or not you are in the presence of an ambitious urinal or a confirmed masterpiece. That's because, if the twentieth century taught us anything worthwhile, it was that the experience of 'art' does not begin and end at the front door of an art gallery or museum. Get it right and you'll be able to enjoy what T.S. Eliot called 'a lifetime burning in every moment'. Or a lifetime peeing in Duchamp's urinal.

But I'm not advocating that an incorporeal mysticism should surround us like an aura as we detach ourselves from the surly bonds that restrain us to Earth. On the contrary: I love the world of things, urinals included. Being able to enjoy stuff adds dignity and ceremony to everyday experience.

I learnt this being taken around the factories my father used to manage. Instead of going to football matches as a youth, I spent Saturday afternoons with a Cincinnati four-axis lathe, boggling at the exquisiteness of the aircraft components it made.

You don't have to own a jet to enjoy the beauty of its components. In fact, you might enjoy them even more if you have not actually paid the $100 million (not including discounts) necessary for the purchase of a gorgeous Gulfstream G650ER. But if a business jet's Power Transfer Unit is not available to admire, there's similar pleasure to be had from contemplating the handsome shoulders of a Burgundy bottle, something which, if at all possible, really should be an everyday experience.

But the world of stuff is under threat; our analogue age is coming to an end, or, at least, its development is stalling. Virtual experiences are succeeding material ones. Put it this way: the richest man in the world doesn't make things; he owns a delivery business powered by vast server farms pumping yet more heat into an already scorched Arizona desert.

If you asked Amazon to deliver a urinal in the style of Marcel Duchamp, there's no doubt it could, but if you asked Jeff Bezos how it was made, I suspect he would not have a clue. We seem to be losing our grip on things.

But, personally, never mind urinal art and aerospace componentry, I'd rather look at a bowl of fruit (especially lemons) than strap on a virtual-reality headset and 'enjoy' telematic sex, following erotic dynamics determined not by individual passion, but by a coding nerd with scrofula and a novelty T-shirt.

The very day I am writing this, a news site is trumpeting 'Microsoft puts the whole world in a game'. Oh, dear me, please don't let this be true. I don't want the world to become a game with a set of instructions drafted by another coding nerd. I'd like the world to preserve mystery, curiosity, fear, accident, discovery, personality, privacy, privilege, idiosyncrasy, choice, bloody-mindedness, chance. Mistakes and flaws are so much more interesting than perfection. And perfect knowledge does not exist. Doubt is, in any case, surely more interesting than certainty.

At the same time, the world of ideas is similarly threatened. It's not that we are short of data: there are lots of people out there who are much too busy measuring the height of tables and producing redundant data in woeful abundance. But we are short of genuine information, of idiosyncratic opinion. Information is data sent on imaginative vectors, adding value to mere facts. And 'imagination'?

Victor Hugo said it was 'intelligence with an erection', which sounds like a very good thing. Instead of this, there is a limp, melancholy and deadly tendency towards collective thought.

One remedy for the digitalisation of experience is to understand and take pleasure in tangible, everyday things, to engage with the mystery of the ordinary. Victor Hugo again: 'to love someone is to see the face of God'. I have been thinking the face of God can be seen on more occasions than is conventionally assumed.

The subtitle here may be misleading, because – while it costs nothing to enjoy the feeling of rain on your face – you do, of course, need a little money to travel and see and acquire stuff. L'abbaye du Thoronet is, for example, not going to come to you. Nor, alas, is the Prado going to lend you a Velázquez.

There's no argument here against money and its expression in consumerism, just against the wrong sort of consumerism. Patiently acquiring a personal collection of, say, Duralex glasses is a fine thing. This is because they are an example of excellence in design, being elegant, useful, indestructible and timeless – all valuable properties. The wrong sort of consumerism is, for example, the brainless neophilia of the fashion cycle . . . perhaps now nearing its end as more people appreciate enduring qualities rather than momentary ones.

My sources are as follows. I have met a great many of the world's (perhaps more accurately 'the last century's') leading architects and designers. For instance: Raymond Loewy, Dieter Rams, Richard Rogers, Saul Bass, Milton Glaser, Ettore Sottsass, Achille Castiglioni, Philip Johnson, Giorgetto Giugiaro, Mario Bellini, F.A. Porsche, Verner Panton, Jony Ive. Architects and designers can be affected and annoying, but they are people who have patiently negotiated an understanding of the material world. More so than most.

The great thing about architects and designers is that their calling positively requires them to have views. You can't, for example, take on the task of designing someone's home without having opinions about the values of domesticity and how life should be lived.

A designer looks at the world and thinks: this is pretty interesting. And then a second thought occurs: perhaps I could do it a little better. Maybe next he shrugs and concedes that it's pretty interesting anyway. The designer has an *aesthetic* view of existence, a conviction that appearances really do matter.

And designers acquire opinions about the philosophy of existence too, although not many of them put it exactly that way. The graphic designer Milton Glaser – the one who hearted New York so memorably – once told me, unforgettably, that conversations about value and quality would be very much easier and greatly improved if we replaced the word 'art' with the word 'work'. This was because 'art' carries so many rarefied expectations, while 'work' is nicely down to earth.

And there's more. I have been to an awful lot of cities, very many interesting restaurants and hotels, seen most of the world's great buildings and great art . . . at least in the Western canon. You learn by listening and looking. And what follows is what I have learnt from these people, these places and these pictures.

All art forms are commentaries on and criticisms of existence. And that goes for the painting of altarpieces or the design of a potato peeler that works properly. I am enchanted by the meaning of things, of how ordinary stuff can have emotional value. But now there's even more.

Here's what I believe: you can design your own life to be a

performance, and you can become your own critic. You can surround yourself with stuff you understand and admire. You can learn to read and enjoy the world.

As Eric Gill – stonemason, sculptor, typographer, zoologically inspired fornicator, a man who knew his dogs – understood, the artist is not a different sort of person. Every person is a different sort of artist. Or, at least, they can be with a little repurposing.

Value is about the pleasure to be had from the ordinary and the everyday. But it is also about appreciating beauty in material things, about having an entirely *aesthetic* view of the world, like a designer. And it is in favour of the argument about the primacy of the analogue over the digital and virtual: the most analogue things in the world are buildings, paintings and food. They are not going digital any time soon.

But there are intangibles that are valuable too. Personal charm cannot be measured but can always be detected. Charm is worth cultivating in yourself and encouraging in others. And if it seems incongruous to discuss insubstantial gods and ghosts in a book about solid stuff, this is because it's rewarding to think of what's beyond the here and now, as pleasurable as the here and now might be.

The ghosts I believe in are not cartoonish spooks but those indefinable feelings of depth and continuity and mystery which being in touch with material beauty bring. Never forget: anything that is made betrays the beliefs and convictions of the people who made it. And these beliefs do not disappear.

When the philosopher Gilbert Ryle coined the expression 'ghost in the machine' in 1949, he was thinking of the mind–body dichotomy. But I'll steal it here to describe the secret meaning of things. Everything and everywhere are haunted.

No one could express it better than Roland Barthes, so I will not even try. Here is the fastidious Sorbonne professor proclaiming his astonishment at the beautiful new Citroën he saw at the 1955 Salon de l'Automobile in Paris:

Il ne faut pas oublier que l'objet est le meilleur messager de la surnature: il y a facilement dans l'objet, à la fois une perfection et une absence d'origine, une clôture et une brillance, une transformation de la vie en matière (la matière est bien plus magique que la vie), et pour tout dire un silence qui appartient à l'ordre du merveilleux.

(We must not forget that an object is the best messenger of a world above that of nature: one can easily see in an object at once a perfection and an absence of origin, a closure and a brilliance, a transformation of life into matter (matter is much more magical than life), and in a word a silence which belongs to the realm of fairy-tales.) This was published in Barthes' collection of essays *Mythologies* (1957).

My ghosts are these 'best messengers'. They bring value to the party.

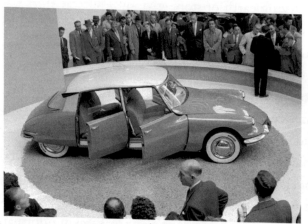

STF/Getty Images

The sight of this beautiful car at the 1955 Salon de l'Automobile in Paris moved Roland Barthes, pioneer semiotician, to declare that design was 'the best messenger of a world superior to Nature'.

The Great Isolation
What do I really want?

It's a coincidence that this book was written during a period when the world was astonished into a state of unprecedented disruption.

After a big storm, the air begins to clear.

And when a landscape – or a cityscape – drenched with rain begins to dry in the sun, there is a unique smell in the atmosphere. Drying earth or stone give off a special aroma, a little bit musty, but otherwise indefinable other than being very evocative . . . of I don't know quite what. Beautiful, even.

My own guess is that this smell short-circuits the intellect and takes us directly back to a prehistoric moment when Fred Flintstone realised the worst of the thunder and lightning was over and it was safe to leave the cave. He put his head over the threshold, sniffed the air and thought, 'This is good.' And then he went clubbing.

The part of the brain that processes smell is close to the part that processes memory, so some leakage of information is entirely possible. Sniffing the air, Fred realised this was a good moment to start again.

This smell was named 'petrichor' by two Australian scientists in 1964. Of course, it had been around for ever, but identifying it with a name created a new awareness. The 'petr' bit means stone and 'ichor' is the animating fluid that flows through the veins of the gods. Important stuff. We need more divine animation, not less.

In the most general sense, a lot of people are smelling petrichor right now. And people are asking the simple – but really quite profound – question: how is it best to *spend* time? And they are not all thinking of consulting the tachymetric rim-scale of your chronometer expensively sourced at Watches of Switzerland.

There is a conventional distinction between mechanical time and cosmic time. The former is what the clocks and calendars tell us, and they are cruel masters and accurate only in a simple sense. The latter is the natural rhythm of things.

But during what will surely become known as 'The Great Isolation', mechanical time became almost irrelevant. Mechanical time is, however, a recent invention. It was only in the nineteenth century when railway companies became concerned about trains following different schedules onto a deadly 'collison course' that a need arose for universal coordinated time.

Contributing to the recent marginalisation of mechanical time, no one listened to broadcast news on the hour during The Great Isolation and rigid TV schedules gave way to the pleasant anarchy of streaming. Tuesday blurred and bled into Wednesday and March blurred into April and summer into autumn. Most of us found ourselves, unwittingly, but I think often quite happily, on cosmic time.

Time lost its shape as days and weeks and months blurred into each other. No edges, no beginnings and no ends. Lunch was cancelled, deadlines evaporated, party invitations disappeared like spit on a hot griddle, schedules became irrelevant, people's diaries were empty. Future social historians will marvel at the fact that in most of 2020 nobody made any appointments with anyone. No one evidently did anything. It was one long Blursday.

Coming out of The Great Isolation and into the light, people began to sniff the air and start again. People were asking, 'What do I really want?' This is a traditional philosophical enquiry which put the *New York Times*'s distinguished film critic A.O. Scott into what he called a nagging, wandering paralysis. Must we leave it to Netflix and Amazon to satisfy our every appetite?

Interestingly, deadly infestation and strategies to escape or recover from it are recurrent events in history. Plagues are not rarities in human affairs; they are the norm.

In 1353, the Tuscan poet Giovanni Bocaccio wrote *The Decameron*, a hundred often bawdy tales set against a background where Florence had been infected by the Black Death. One episode in *The Decameron* involves seven young women and three young men refusing to stay at home and fleeing to the safety of the suburbs, leaving a lot of anxious urbanites trapped inside the city's ancient walls. Here, oblivious to the suffering left behind, once in the country, everyone became king or queen . . . if only for a day. These are now familiar dreams.

'The spirits of the company rose, and they seasoned their viands with pleasant jests and sprightly sallies.'

Giovanni Bocaccio

Then there is Alessandro Manzoni's *I Promessi Sposi* of 1827, the 'Great Italian Novel', which describes the Milan infestation of 1630. The circumstances now sound strikingly familiar: **'While officialdom was delving for the truth, the man in the street, as often happens, was in full possession of it.'**

Or take the German–Jewish poet Heinrich Heine, who wrote journalism of shocking clarity about the Paris plague of 1832. And George Eliot's *Romola*, a novel of 1862, is set in Florence during the life of the heretic priest Savonarola, who was burnt at the stake in 1498. Sent to deal with Jewish plague victims, the heroine Romola finds her appetite for life healthily refreshed by the surrounding devastation and death. There is, as Confucius knew, nothing quite so pleasing, metaphorically speaking, as watching a friend fall off a roof.

My favourite example of 'Contagion Lit', however, is Jack London's adventure yarn *The Scarlet Plague*, set in 2073, sixty years after an infestation originating in San Francisco killed everyone except the ingenious survivors who flew to Hawaii on airships.

But the consummate masterpiece of the genre is Thomas Mann's novella *Death in Venice*, published in 1912, the same year as *The Scarlet Plague*. To illustrate the moral ambiguity excited by epidemics, Gustav von Aschenbach refuses to leave a Venice infested with cholera because he has a homoerotic, paedophiliac fixation on a pretty Polish boy called Tadzio. Von Aschenbach becomes sunk in the 'voluptuousness of doom', as many of us have so very recently. But von Aschenbach experienced a peculiar and even delicious sense of pleasure at his dire predicament: he was caught – suspended – between temporary lust and permanent extinction.

And the threat of death, as ever, heightened the senses. From his deckchair on The Lido, the doomed old man found Venice 'suspiciously beautiful'. Alas, he did not survive to consummate anything with Tadzio, nor to smell the petrichor. But fear does sharpen the senses.

We can see clearly now the rain has gone. And one thing that is visible with startling clarity is how all forecasts of where we were going have been wrong. No one expects economists to have the skills of epidemiologists, but for all their charts and programmes, their annoying percentages and baffling algorithms, the forecasters did not have second sight. They did not even have first sight.

No economist even predicted the crash of 2008, but anyone who could count and knew how banks worked could see it coming. It was in plain sight. And here's a laughably egregious error: John Maynard Keynes said that by about now we would all be so rich that work would be irrelevant. And what has happened is record unemployment, widespread bankruptcies, business models put into the crusher, institutions in peril and the entire world in a state of shocked dismay.

Economics is not even as accurate as weather forecasting: economists use their awful jargon – 'subjective utility' – to dignify guesswork. The quasi-scientific terms add only a spurious precision.

You can aggregate Crisis Theory, Laffer Curves, Diminishing Marginal Utility, Ricardian Equivalence, Neo Malthusianism, Resource Scarcity, Kondratiev's Waves, Ramsey Numbers and Circular Cumulative Causation, and they count for little, perhaps not even a positive value at all, when compared with the most modest thought of a great poet. John Keats, for example.

'I am certain of nothing but the holiness of the heart's affection and the truth of imagination.'

John Keats

At least Keynes had the decency to admit the inclination of his discipline towards error. 'Economists,' he said, 'set themselves too easy, too useless, a task if in tempestuous seasons they can only tell us that when the storm is long past, the ocean is flat again.' Nor did Keynes live long enough to sniff the petrichor.

The virus exposed the fragility not just of our supply chains (which led to a tragic shortage of medicines and surgical masks) but of our entire belief systems (which led to a dire shortage of knowing what to think).

Economists are the ones who measure the height of a table and expect to determine the future of furniture design by this metric. These measurements provide a spurious precision which has always proved useless at understanding the vagaries of human behaviour. Nor had economists offered much help in dealing with the effect of unanticipated catastrophes, although if more of them had read *The Decameron*, Manzoni, Heine or Mann that might have made a difference.

We have been at the edge of the abyss before. There is a wonderful observation of Einstein's made in a 1949 edition of *Liberal Judaism*: 'I do not know with what weapons World War III will be fought, but World War IV will be fought with sticks and stones.' Fear of calamity and oblivion is not attached uniquely to the millennium and to viruses. When I was a child, we were sent home from school because the Cuban

Missile Crisis made nuclear obliteration just one duff political decision away. I think we were told to hide under the table, not that furniture provided much protection from infernal blasts, stupefying shockwaves, vaporisation and, if you were still blinking, subsequent deadly radiation.

'The lamps are going out all over Europe; we shall not see them lit again in our lifetime.'

Foreign Secretary Edward Grey's words on 3 August 1914, the eve of the First World War. Grey was looking from his Foreign Office window as a lamplighter solemnly did his rounds on The Mall

---

But there was something almost comfortingly finite about Cold War weaponry, no matter how terrifying and evil and murderous. The recent abyss has been very different in character, because levels of uncertainty have been higher. At least you know where you are with an H-bomb. Our Plague made everything feel precarious.

No one was under the gun . . . or under the bomb. But people also began to develop a keen awareness of personal priorities, of how best to extract value from experience.

Holidays suddenly became as mysterious and remote as the domestic habits of the Plantagenets. But how tragic to have holidays kept in reserve: the two weeks of liberty and hedonism allowed against a life of heartless and purposeless drudgery. Why restrict the exhilarating pleasures of a holiday to a mere fourteen days a year?

Valuable Holiday Activities

Readers of Robert Burton's *Anatomie of Melancholie* learn that, *circa* 1621, a holiday might comprise: ringing, bowling, shooting, playing with keel pins, quoits, hurling, wrestling, leaping, fencing, swimming, football and balloons. These were officially endorsed by James I, who criticised the 'Puritans and precise people' who avoided these entertainments. Additionally, at St Bartholomew's Fair, a famous London holiday, Samuel Pepys found monkeys dancing on sticks, which, quite correctly, he found strange.

The nineteenth-century holiday was one of the original consumer products, rivalled only by the creation of the first restaurants in Paris in the eighteenth century as an influence on our expectations, still with us today. Each provided a sort of theatre, a relief from *tedium vitae.*

And as with all consumer products, the holiday experience begs questions of taste and desire. What exactly is on offer? An escape from suburban boredom? A glimpse of a past (or future) Eden? A release from dehumanised toil? Perhaps all of these.

Whatever, whether Scarborough in 1860 or Torremolinos a century later, the former accessed by train, the latter by the first jets, a holiday offered experiences more rare and valuable than those normally available every day. Notably, sex, drink and freedom. Or, at least, pleasing suggestions of them ... made the more tantalising because they were so evidently enjoyed on a very short lease. But why not extend your tenure of summer? The holiday mentality can transcend a fortnight on the Costa Brava and, given the right approach, is available for fifty-two weeks a year.

Despite the fret and anxiety, many people found the

disciplines and constraints and privations of The Great Isolation positively stimulating even as they were disturbing. Great comfort was discovered in domestic ritual. Despite the anxieties and doubts, was this perhaps a Golden Age when real truths were revealed and many false gods were shamefully exposed? The god of travel, a shifty and dissatisfied deity inclined to snare us with lascivious, but nugatory, temptations, was one of them.

People found, often to their surprise, that near horizons can be as interesting as distant ones. Warren Buffett once said that when the tide goes out, you can see who has been swimming naked. In this argument, the naked swimmers would be the airlines, especially the *budget* airlines, the package-tour operators, cruise-ship companies and everybody else in the cynical and deadly conspiracy to ruin destinations with over-tourism.

Travel will never be quite the same again. It may very well be better. One unanticipated benefit of reorganising airports for hygienic protocols, for example, is that they will, perforce, have to become better places to be. If the transit time through an airport doubles from two hours to four, people will demand that those four hours are more civilised and comfortable. Clever architects are onto this already.

Of travel, we will have less, but better. It will be more expensive, but much more valuable. Wasn't it one of the great delusions of the era now passed that travel is *necessarily* enjoyable? Gatwick South Terminal at five-thirty on a February morning? What fresh hell is this?

So much foreign travel has declined from being a romantic privilege to becoming a demeaning and harrowing ordeal. Whether for business or pleasure, we now know that a lot of travel can be done in the head. And at home.

Every Day Is All We've Got
So make it perfect

It was counter-culture heroine Joan Didion, author of 1968's *Slouching Towards Bethlehem*, who memorably explained to a journalist visiting her Park Avenue apartment who was curious and flabbergasted about the everyday custom of, after a morning writing at her desk, lunching alone off fresh white linen and Baccarat crystal.

'Do you do this every day?' the journalist asked.

'Every day is all we've got,' the writer replied without blinking.

'Style is character.'

Joan Didion, *Paris Review* (1978)

If it is true that every day is infinitely precious, an exquisite opportunity to be choreographed and enjoyed, then it's surely important to be certain that everyday things are as good as they can possibly be and we should make the very best of it.

Or think like James Dean, who, ever so briefly, made a religion of glamorous delinquency: dream like you will live for ever; live as if you will die tomorrow. Of course, Dean died aged twenty-four in his Porsche, rather before his dreams had fully formulated themselves.

The beauty and fragility of experience are our persistent preoccupations: every day might be our last. In Les Orres, now a ski resort in the Dauphine, the inscription on an ancient sundial says, *'Quelle heure est-il? Peut-être la mienne'*. Or, 'What time is it? Perhaps your hour has come'. Who does not feel a delicious thrill of horror on reading that? The thought of death, the evidence suggests, concentrates the mind wonderfully.

John Gay, author of the 1728 *Beggar's Opera*, was keenly aware of optimising the present moment. Whatever are the alternatives to making the very best of it? Procrastination is lazy and only suited to the terminally unimaginative. On his epitaph in Westminster Abbey, Gay predicted the disappointments of not being alive.

'Life is jest, and all things show it; I thought it once, but now I know it!'

John Gay's epitaph

Engaging with the immediacy of the everyday happily entails the rediscovery of simple pleasures: the satisfaction of rituals, the luxury of the senses, the enjoyment of the ordinary, the almost sensual thrill of free intellectual enquiry into the whole range from 'ecstasy to pathos' which, given the right attitude, can be enjoyed without leaving your kitchen.

If you want to enjoy the ordinary, join the queue.

How to Enjoy a Queue

Maybe we will even have learnt to take pleasure in queuing – given the right attitude, the most banal activity can become edifying. As architect Ben Pentreath explained, talking of student life in suboptimal lodgings, 'waiting for the hot-water to heat up again is when the best conversations happen'. To enjoy a queue, you need a fine mixture of stoicism, curiosity, tolerance and whatever is the opposite of pride. Thus, a healthy mixture. To queue is to accept the existence of hierarchy and order and to profess their superiority over brute selfishness and anarchy. A queue is about shared interests. Sartre said that in a queue we 'achieve practical and theoretical participation in common being'. And what could be more fascinating than decoding the contents of someone else's supermarket trolley? In a classic academic paper of 1978, the social psychologist Barry Schwartz described the queue as a process and said that 'life is a confrontation between the individual and a world of naturally infinite tasks'. Like being on the top of a bus, a queue is not dead time, but a fine opportunity to scrutinise civilisation.

Routine commentary on The Great Isolation cited Daniel Defoe's *Journal of the Plague Year* (1722), but his earlier and better-known *Robinson Crusoe* (1719) has more interesting insights into such a predicament. The shipwrecked Crusoe – based on a real historical figure – spent twenty years in involuntary isolation, sheltering in place on what's now identified as Juan Fernández Island in the Caribbean, near Venezuela.

'I looked upon the world as a thing remote . . . a place I had lived in, but was come out of it,' Crusoe says, a feeling the furloughed and threatened and isolated might readily understand.

Crusoe maintained his dignity in isolation, kept busy and made himself a fur suit and a fur hat provided by animals he had hunted. He also made an umbrella. He did not surrender to self-pity or despair on his lonely island, but kept himself industrious, curious and alert.

'Thus I lived mighty comfortably, my mind being entirely composed by resigning myself to the will of God and throwing myself wholly on the disposal of His providence. This made my life better than sociable, for when I began to regret the want of conversation I would ask myself whether thus conversing mutually with my own thoughts, and (as I hope I may say) even with God Himself, by ejaculations was not better than the utmost enjoyment of human society in the world?'

Robinson Crusoe

Not for nothing is Robinson Crusoe the dedicatee of this book.

Universal History Archive/Getty Images

Daniel Defoe's Robinson Crusoe was the prototype castaway: an individual who had known civilization, but was painfully removed from it. Crusoe's remedies for his plight remain moving and relevant today.

Catastrophe at the Met Gala
Beware of any enterprise requiring new clothes

J.K. Galbraith, a liberal adviser to the Kennedys, wrote in *The Affluent Society* (1958) that we are 'excessively organised for unimportant purposes'.

Fashion is one of the most unimportant purposes of them all. It was once neatly described as buying stuff you don't need with money you don't have to impress people you don't like.

Anyone who has seen New York's Met Gala, a fashion zoo or the Monaco Influencers' festival of brainless kitsch or visited a so-called 'VIP Club' has seen an atrocious conga line of primped and preened suck-holes, pathetically credulous strivers chasing the falsest of false gods in an overlit Satanic game show for the overdressed and under-scrupulous.

Here's a debased culture where credibility is calibrated by Twitter traffic. In a VIP Club, whales and mooks, as the punters are so disagreeably called, spend $40,000 on a 'bottle of Dom'. In one Los Angeles VIP Club, your $40,000 bottle of Dom is delivered to your table by midgets, suspended from cables, apparently flying through the perfumed, but sordid, air.

The Met Gala is a spectacle of such unrestrained venality it might make a debauched Rococo dilettante, never mind a recovering Puritan, sick. What's the old saying? I wanted a long-term relationship with fame but ended up on a one-night stand with the frazzled whore that is celebrity. Pornography? You need a bigger and more condemnatory word.

The Potlatch Ceremony

Expensive clubs and celebrity events like the Met Gala have been compared by anthropologists to the potlatch ceremonies of the north-west Canada first nation people. A potlatch is a feast of gift giving, a ceremony dedicated to excess. Candles, canoes, dried fish and so on. But the gifts must be destroyed to demonstrate the power of the host. This ritual of wealth destruction was illegal – on grounds of wastefulness – between 1884 and 1951.

The awful irony is, the founders of the Metropolitan Museum were New York's leading philanthropists and artists of 1870. Their terrible progeny comprises the tone-deaf rich, their pilot fish, preening publicists, credulous hangers-on, predatory media and terminal show-offs. Value destroyers all.

The Met Gala theme of 2020 was to have been 'reimagining fashion history'. But the event was cancelled. No need, really, to reimagine fashion history – circumstances are doing it for us. Like travel, another thing that is going to change is fashion. When death threatens to stalk the catwalk alongside leggy zonked-out models, a new Gucci handbag does not, perhaps, seem quite so important as it once did.

In his 2020 memoir *Intelligence for Dummies*, Andy Warhol's old associate Glenn O'Brien had a nice description of a glossy high-fashion ad, the sort whose presence in the magazine paid for *Vogue* editor Anna Wintour's hairdos (her Park Avenue helmet): 'Two five-figure hookers on a bed, on drugs, one passed-out in a garter belt showing her complete arse and the other making goofball eye-contact with the reader.'

This is the goofball value system you buy into when shopping on Bond Street, Rodeo Drive or avenue Montaigne. It's a horrible conspiracy of confected desire organised by a handful of global 'luxury goods' businesses and their always compliant poodles in the old and new media.

And then there is the fine principle John Ruskin made famous: you can count yourself rich by what you can do without (although this same notion has been recurrent in European thought since Seneca).

John Ruskin

John Ruskin (1819–1900) was not just the greatest art critic of the nineteenth century, he was the greatest art critic ever. Or certainly the most influential. He was a ganglion of contradictions: Ruskin supported the hazy paintings of Turner but attacked the hazy paintings of Whistler. He despised and feared industry (especially reciprocating engines, possibly because they reminded him of sex, of which he was also fearful) but loved science. Especially geology and minerology. However, his great achievement, realised with absolute consistency, was to see that anything that is made betrays the beliefs of the person who makes it. In about 1860, with the publication of

Unto This Last, one of the most beautiful polemics ever written, he turned away from straightforward criticism of art and
architecture and towards political economy. He believed that
carving a bracket in *pietra serena* was at least as important as
painting a masterpiece. Members of Ruskin's Guild of St
George did road mending and road sweeping. Eventually, he
went mad. Ruskin influenced Marcel Proust, Mahatma Gandhi
(who translated *Unto This Last* into Gujurati), the Labour Party
and the Greens.

Amuse yourself by wondering what John Ruskin – that
'exemplum of mankind', according to Marcel Proust – would
have to say about a handbag costing £5,000. Its maker so
detached from meaningful labour, its user so proud and vain
and heartless.

'There is nothing in the world of which he is not capable; he
loves and desires everything and after having possessed all,
he knows how to make out with nothing.'

The Prince de Ligne on Casanova in
Mélanges anecdotiques littéraires et politiques (1835)

Interestingly, during The Great Isolation, people became
especially sensitive to resources and waste and sceptical about
the perverse and glossy sheen of the fashion business's ads. I
say 'business' rather than 'industry', because the latter word
still contains suggestions of dignity and purpose. And honest
toil. Fashion is a money business, and money does not talk,
it swears.

On average, it's estimated a fast-fashion garment is worn only seven times before it is thrown away. Clothing industries consume about 25 per cent of global chemical production. Seven hundred gallons of water are required to grow the cotton for a single T-shirt. In Xintang, in China's Guandong province, there are *three thousand* factories manufacturing 800,000 pairs of jeans a day. The toxic run-off has killed the local river.

But I'd be the last one to argue that appearances are unimportant. As Lord Chesterfield wrote to his errant son while on the Grand Tour, dress is a very foolish thing, but it is a very foolish thing not to be well dressed. Getting dressed appropriately for context is a civilised challenge difficult to ignore.

Meanwhile, at home, during The Great Isolation, dress codes went in violently different directions. One incarcerated friend proudly reported on spending entire days in rotting damask dressing-gowns, altering this seedy costume only to climb into gangrenous corduroy bags and a moth-eaten cashmere jumper. Another friend, in remote Norfolk, became very interested in wardrobe rotation. I prefer this latter route, since it conforms to that old definition of a gentleman being someone who is polite when it is not necessarily an advantage to be so.

My gentleman reported buying used Edward Green monk shoes (about £1,200), a Cody Wellema hat, handmade Neapolitan shirts by Luca Avitabile and silk ties from Schostal, an exclusive outfitter in Rome, this all to be worn when no one might see him. He became concerned about the propriety of a cream versus a white shirt, especially if made in needle-cord.

He knows that a wardrobe of finely weathered and textured shoes, all repeatedly repaired, is a source of deep satisfaction. Good shoes, skilfully repaired, are not mere footwear, they are a wearable philosophy. If it can be repaired, repair it.

And never forget Henry David Thoreau's advice to **'Beware of any enterprise requiring *new* clothes'**. This discomfort about novelty was a High Victorian puritanism shared with John Ruskin: a belief in the dignity of labour, the spirituality of things, the morality of art and architecture, the way things whisper stories about you.

That 'newness' may be morally dubious is the underlying theme of Holman Hunt's *Awakening Conscience*, an 1854 painting in Tate Britain which is a fine expression of confused Victorian sensibility. A 'kept-woman' (the female reduced to the condition of a chattel) sits on the knees of her keeper, who is, in turn, sitting on a piano stool. He is fingering the keyboard (and soon, doubtless, expects to be fingering her) when a chance note struck on the keyboard hits one of her neural colonies, awakening her hitherto dormant conscience. She is pictured just at the moment of rising up from her debased position, suddenly enlightened and freed.

Ruskin, reviewing the Royal Academy exhibition where the painting was first shown, said you knew the man to be a cad not because of his lecherous expression, but because of the 'fatal newness' of the furniture. Only someone immoral would buy his own piano. The sort of man who buys his own furniture was, in this reading, not to be trusted.

John Ruskin Q&A

Q. Why do we work?

A. The highest reward for a person is not what they get for their work, but what they become by it.

Q. What's wrong with travel?

A. Modern travelling is not travelling at all; it is merely being sent to a place, and very little different from being a parcel.

Q. How do you determine the value of something?

A. A thing is worth what it can do for you, not what you choose to pay for it.

Q. Are you a rich man?

A. It is not how much one makes, but to what purpose one spends.

Ruskin's doubts about a new piano as well as Thoreau's doubts about new clothes were not simply based in penny-pinching frugality, although there was probably a bit of that. There was

London Stereoscopic Company/Stringer/ Getty Images

The Victorians demanded moral certainties. In orotund, Biblical cadences, John Ruskin provided them. Moving from art criticism to social analysis, he demanded the ultimate respect for dignified manual labour. Ruskin believed that 'the desire for beauty is the path that leads us to the people we love'.

also a high-caste belief that wearing old clothes is an act of magnificent hauteur, since it suggests that the wearer has both dignity to spare and better things to think about. And inheriting old furniture shows you have *class* because you have forebears. It was a test at Victorian public school to ask pupils if they knew the names of their great-grandparents. If you like this sort of thing, trust me, this test is infallible.

Still, there are other important questions to be asked about what we wear other than how new it is. Fashion may be going out of fashion, but how to be well dressed is a continuing everyday question which will be asked long after fast fashion has died an ignominious death.

While it is true that during The Great Isolation the wearing of a suit made you look suspiciously like a chauffeur, an interest in being well-presented is a mark of character. And finding the answer to what 'well-presented' actually means is satisfying. Must socks match the colour of the shoe or the trouser? Should a Donegal Tweed jacket sourced on eBay be lined or unlined? My dress-obsessed friend and I had a long exchange about whether suit trousers should have belt loops. In this febrile intellectual atmosphere, buttons became something of an obsession. But this is something that concerned Andy Warhol too. At a fashion shoot, where the glitz was laid on so heavily you couldn't cut it with a chainsaw, Warhol asked the photographer David Bailey in his magnificently downbeat deflationary style, 'Do you ever think about all the people that make buttons?' Unhappily, Bailey's reply is not recorded.

If God really is in the details, and maybe He is, then buttons are Holy. Here is wonderful evidence. If you become interested in buttons (an adventure I heartily endorse), you can start by fretting whether they should have two holes or four. And you will soon learn that button sizes are determined by the ancient French measurement of *ligne*.

Of course, every fool knows that the buttons on the shirt cuff, the *plaquet* and the jacket should be different sizes. Just as Francis Galton knew there was a right and a wrong way of rolling up shirt sleeves. And, as the tailors say, when it comes to jacket buttons, should it be 'three show two' or 'four show three'?

How to Judge a Suit

Generally, it is about attention to detail . . . which is, depending in your view, where either God or the Devil reside.

Buttons, of course. Note number and materials.

Glossiness and brightness rarely good. In a magnificently snobbish conceit, the critic Paul Fussell says, 'You can gauge people's proximity to prole status by the colour and polyester content of their garments.'

And in anything other than summer, a really good suit will have a supportive canvased lining.

The fit of the arm hole is a dead giveaway.

But most deadly of all is what Fussell calls 'prole gape': that chasm at the back of the neck between shirt and suit collar. It is never present on a properly cut suit.

Check the purity of the pocket apertures.

Puckering – anywhere – is not good.

Fast fashion? Absolutely not. We need to save Chinese rivers. New clothes? Not necessarily. Care and precision in dress? Most certainly. If all the above seems close to religiose obsessiveness, that is probably the point. You can judge a man by his buttons. In a suit with a three-button jacket, you may sometimes have the top button done up. The middle one, always. The bottom one never. A man with the bottom button of his suit jacket done up must immediately be under suspicion.

Horn or plastic? You must by now know the answer.

Lunch and Dinner
The benefits of myopia

What we have all had to do – whether or not we are button fanciers or subscribers to popular psychological cults – when faced with a nasty disease that seems, or seemed, all but out of control, is to become 'mindful'.

The belief that being in the present is the best place to be is a recurrent one in wise people from Marcus Aurelius, the 'Philosopher Emperor', to Jorge Luis Borges, the blind Argentinian librarian and professional fantasist. Borges advised us always to remember that the present moment is indefinite because the past is a present memory and the future is a present hope. It is, after all, memory of the past and fear of the future which create the majority of anxiety: 'good health and a bad memory' was Ingrid Bergman's recipe for happiness.

'Consider that as the heaps of sand piled on one another hide the former sands, so in life the events which go before are soon covered by those which come after.'

Marcus Aurelius

And the mindfulness idea was becoming well known in the nineteenth century. My favourite example is 'the key to happiness is to think no further ahead than lunch or dinner', my paraphrase of the excellent Sidney Smith, of whom more below.

The plans involved in making lunch become engrossing: deciding on what to eat, sourcing the ingredients, preparing the dish and, of course, eating it in good company (or, alternatively, in contemplative solitude, which can be just as good). These plans can absorb all the energy available on the emotional bandwidth. And as soon as lunch is over you will need to be making plans for dinner. And so on and so on.

This idea appealed also to James Salter, a fighter pilot, scriptwriter and novelist who is to many one of the very finest prose writers of the late twentieth century. Certainly, his 1997 memoir *Burning the Days* is a strong candidate for a modern classic. Salter led a life of enviable richness: a brave airman, a Pulitzer Prize winner, good company, a generous host and, by all accounts, a loving husband. His was a life very well lived.

Salter's last book was 2014's *Life Is Meals*, this 'food lover's book of days' compiled with his wife. It is a mixture of anecdote and anthology, an account of days spent cooking, travelling, eating and entertaining based on old notebooks collected over the years. 'Life never felt richer', Salter said, than when at the kitchen worktop or the dining table.

This attractive lunch-and-dinner Completion Theory is a version of Sidney Smith's magnificent advice, as true today as it was two hundred years ago, in a letter written to Lady Georgiana Cavendish in 1820. The Reverend Smith was full of sound guidance:

Dear Lady Georgiana,

Nobody has suffered more from low spirits than I have done, so I feel for you.

1st: Live as well as you dare.

2nd: Go into the showerbath with a small quantity of water at a temperature low enough to give you a slight sensation of cold.

3rd: Read amusing books.

4th: Take short views of human life – not further than dinner or tea.

5th: Be as busy as you can.

6th: See as much as you can of those friends who like and respect you.

7th: And of those acquaintances who amuse you.

8th: Make no secret of low spirits to your friends, but talk of them freely – they are always worse for dignified concealment.

9th: Attend to the effects tea and coffee produce upon you.

10th: Don't expect too much from human life – a sorry business at the best.

11th: Compare your lot with that of other people.

12th: Avoid poetry, dramatic representations (except comedy), music, serious novels, melancholy, sentimental people, everything likely to excite feeling or emotion, not ending in active benevolence.

13th: Do good and endeavour to please everybody of every degree.

14th: Be as much as you can in the open air without fatigue.

15th: Make the room where you commonly sit gay and pleasant.

16th: Struggle little by little against idleness.

17th: Don't be too severe upon yourself, or underrate yourself, but do yourself justice.

18th: Keep good blazing fires.

19th: Be firm and constant in the exercise of rational religion.

20th: Believe me, dear Lady Georgiana.

Very truly yours, Sidney Smith.

Fast or Slow?
The mood of humanity

Meanwhile, before it so unpredictably slowed down, our world was too busy. And not in the way the Reverend Smith meant. He was advocating meaningful engagement with useful tasks. But busy people of recent years have too often been committed to unnecessary activity. As soon as they ceased being busy during the global paralysis of 2020, many of them became aware of an awful, nauseating void.

The debate about whether the world needed to be faster or slower is not new. The novelist E.M. Forster had predicted a slowdown a century ago. His astonishing 1909 novella *The Machine Stops* describes what happens when a future civilisation dependent on machinery discovers that the machinery can fail. We have a similar and perilous dependence on 'tech' today.

On the one side of the fast-or-slow debate, there were frothy-mouthed evangelists and what they called 'The Great Acceleration'. These Great Accelerators were the folk who excitedly referenced Moore's law about computer capacity growing at a geometric rate and to such a point that – stifling now a yawn – Artificial Intelligence exceeds HumInt, or Human Intelligence, really quite soon. People become redundant in a condition which these seers describe as an Orwellian 'singularity', HumInt being a charmless neologism for 'soul'.

This is surely quaint. Great Accelerators have really a lot in common with the rascals who designed and engineered 'planned obsolescence' in the Detroit of the fifties. But at least the advocates of planned obsolescence gave us some gloriously vulgar cars to enjoy. Just look at, say, a '57 Cadillac and marvel at the innocence of a civilisation that found such a thing not only acceptable but positively desirable. **Even as it destroys natural resources in an ungodly manner, it speaks of desire and pleasure . . . which are, of course, natural resources too.**

On the other hand, we find the perhaps more thoughtful advocates of 'degrowth'. That's not an elegant term, but it is an attractive idea: the belief that the real value of any enterprise might be measured not in terms of profit alone, nor of size nor market dominance, but in its ability to endure, to provide stable employment, meaningful and satisfying work, and in its ability to make worthwhile contributions to society and to culture. The dominant global businesses today can make no such claims.

In this context, a Cadillac, for all its absurdities, seems more valuable than Facebook. Harley Earl was the Cadillac's designer. He was chief wizard in the den of kitsch that was Detroit's General Motors in the fifties. And he was better able to test the mood of humanity than Mark Zuckerberg. At least Harley Earl liked his customers, and no one has ever accused the Facebook founder of such a thing. Earl and his accomplices created the iconography of the dynamic economy, literally designing new forms of desire, new expressions of pleasure every year.

While we still have the chance, let's enjoy the automobile, machines with soul and built as an expression of a quaint version of speed. What could be more analogue than being propelled in a metal carriage by a sequence of more or less contained explosions of flammable liquids?

I've Got a Fast Car

Aldous Huxley said that speed was the only experience unique to the modern world. Flight, for example, had been known to the pioneer balloonists of the eighteenth century. At a speed-awareness course in London, the novelist Will Self explained to an astonished instructor, 'I like driving fast because it's fucking fun.' To the philosopher–motorist Matthew B. Crawford, in *Why We Drive* (2020), high speed was exhilarating and life-affirming. He said there was a 'tonic effect in being scared shitless and trusting in your own skills'.

Michel Baret/Getty Images

The excess of Detroit kitsch is obvious. What needs explaining is that a '57 Cadillac might have offended epicene European taste but delivered a thrilling analogue experience to American Dreamers.

Say what you like about the depredations of the oil-burning automobile, now at five minutes to midnight in its life cycle, but the simple pleasure of driving a car is one of the most enthralling analogue experiences.

When Harley Earl said, 'When you get in a car, it should be like going on vacation for a while,' he was referring to the emotionally transformative effects of his chrome and Naugahyde, a notably unpleasant artificial leather named for the rubber town of Naugatuck, Connecticut, and spaceship iconography. And it was a vacation that could be enjoyed every single day, provided you could afford a car . . . as almost everyone in the US at the time could.

Glorious that a machine as crude as a pink Cadillac might have so transformative an effect.

Detroit's was a strange dream world . . . whose passing might be welcomed but is nonetheless tinged with regret. Of course, Detroit's business model of the fifties – which positively *depended* on generating waste – is nearly criminal by the standards of today. But never before had such a large volume of emotional value been created by bashing metal.

In one of his many dystopian reveries, J.G. Ballard speculated that by about 2002 the use of private cars would be restricted to formal 'motoring parks' where driving might be enjoyed only under psychiatric supervision. That has not happened yet. But it might happen soon.

Any experience of driving is, if you attune yourself, emotionally rewarding. You are in charge of a complex and dangerous machine whose explosions are tamed by the thrashing teeth of metal gears and hauled in by the friction materials of the brakes. It is an infernal symphony of heat and noise whose primitive exuberance is only slightly disguised by the cosmetic performative refinements made possible by remedial engineering. You have experienced intercourse with a machine.

But there is another dimension to driving. For all the perils and frustrations of traffic, being on the road is an opportunity for civic display which online activity cannot replicate. Progress in traffic depends on anticipation and sophisticated hand-foot-eye coordination. A car journey is a real-world drama of cultural modelling, status competition and occult sexual display. Satisfyingly, when driving, you depend on your senses and sound judgement to survive.

Driving – fast or slow – may be one of our final freedoms. And it is a gloriously valuable experience ... the more so because it will soon be no more, replaced by electronic transport podules no more engaging than a microwave oven or an internet router or a Kindle. And I think existence will be less rich. A valuable experience will have been lost.

The New Ludd

Why care about an espresso cup?

'Of all dust, the ashes of dead controversies afford the driest.' These are the words of Arthur Quiller-Couch, the man who established, against lively opposition, Eng. Lit. as an academic discipline at Cambridge University.

So, let's maybe be cautious about the value of cold academic, intellectual, technical and forensic scrutiny. Indeed, put them into competition with hotter feelings. 'Value' is a word synonymous with merit, utility, advantage and pleasure. **Value concerns the beliefs, rather than the rules, which govern behaviour.** Value is not about measurement, but about feeling.

Our media dignify irrelevance and trivialise the important. 'What we love will ruin us,' said Neil Postman in his 1985 book *Amusing Ourselves to Death*. It may already have done so. Postman was referring to the seductive delights of television, a twentieth-century device which Clive James called 'the idiot's lantern'. Then in 1992's *Technopoly*, Postman, not a moment too soon, applied his scrutiny to computers, the idiots' lanterns of the century to come.

You do not have to be a technophobe to be alarmed by our daily consumption of clickbait. The phenomenon would have been recognised by B.F. Skinner, the influential behaviourist psychologist, as a sinister sort of manipulation which undermines individual choice.

Skinner coined the term 'operant conditioning'. He described how the behaviour of rats could be designed and directed if they were given rewards after performing certain tasks, a process that he called 'reinforcement'. He created 'Skinner boxes' to study the rats: these were equipped with levers for input and little chutes for rewards. To describe our present predicament, 'rats in a trap' is an expression that readily comes to mind.

Elegiacally, Skinner's scary book *Walden Two* of 1948 referenced Henry David Thoreau's original *Walden* of 1854, a hymn to solitary life in the woods and a hymn to the independent human spirit. Thoreau, as well as being the disdainer of new clothes, is the reference point for finding value in modesty. He reappears here later.

'I had three chairs in my house. One for solitude. Two for friendship. Three for society.'

Henry David Thoreau

Now there is a coming sensibility concerned with the recovery and rediscovery of permanent values lost, or neglected, in the hotshot digital frenzy, the Zuckerberg era, when one of the most influential and dangerous men on the planet wears sweatpants.

Ever so tentatively, people are beginning to glimpse older values as they emerge from an encompassing and disorientating digital fog.

The Neo-Luddite Belief System

The semi-mythical Ned Ludd was a turbulent Leicestershire youth who made a name for himself by smashing mechanised stocking frames in a fit of passion against industrialisation. Today, he would be saying: maps are better than sat-nav, leather (or wool) shoes are better than trainers made from petrochemical byproducts, letters are better than email, postcards are better than Instagram, conversations are better than Twitter, books are better than e-readers, style is better than fashion, trains are better than planes, slow food is better than fast food, history is better than futurism, high street is better than hyperstore, privacy is better than connectivity, walking is better than driving, home is better than abroad, notebooks are better than iPhones, film cameras are better than digital, vinyl is better than Spotify, cinema is better than streaming.

Consider the sedate, old, tethered landline and the promiscuous mobile phone. The latter is peremptory, intrusive and facile. By contrast, a landline had an almost religious aspect. Often it was set on a table in a distant part of a cold entrance hall in the days before central heating. Using a landline required forethought and commitment. It was a ponderous business, but a serious one as well. Landlines did not encourage nuisance or frivolity.

Or what about Instagram versus the postcard? Instagram killed this beautiful medium. The disciplines of selecting images and writing a meaningful message in a space no bigger than two inches by three inches often produced miniature vernacular masterpieces which became precious souvenirs.

The uncomfortable truth is, most people do not know how to live. Netflix certainly helped during The Great Isolation, but streamed movies only get you so far. There's a way to go further, to get beyond a morose and deadly acquiescence before electro-luminescent screens.

We have confronted a global fit of fear and anxiety. In this fretful context, what's the point of caring about the design of an espresso cup?

Here's exactly what. The pleasure to be had from a well-conceived cup, both useful and beautiful and made of fine materials, is an enduring one. And if it is a pleasure that can be enjoyed every day, so much the better. In this context, familiarity breeds respect. Who wants to argue against everyday pleasure? Certainly not me.

And the wonderful thing is, your well-designed espresso cup need not cost a lot. Beauty and efficiency are not expensive, at least not in cash terms.

'Anything that just costs money is cheap.'

Attributed to John Steinbeck

Zen and the Art of Sweeping the Floor
The beauty in banality

The sacred reference point for the modern study of humble rituals is Robert M. Pirsig's *Zen and the Art of Motorcycle Maintenance*. Subtitled 'An Inquiry into Values', Pirsig's *Zen* was published in 1974, an indefinable mixture of novel, travel diary, philosophical meditation and workshop manual, it was at the same time baffling, otiose, prolix and unforgettably original.

It is a book that was rejected 121 times before being accepted for publication.

Pirsig, an academic at a minor US college who had a history of psychiatric troubles, goes on a two-wheeled road trip. The motif of motorcycle maintenance is a device which allows Pirsig to argue that an intense commitment to banalities is rewarding. The mood he creates is a curious combination of trance, philosophy seminar and travel journalism.

There is, in the purely technical sense, not a lot about motorcycle maintenance, although there are wonderful passages about attending to the improvised fabrication of a shim, a sort of washer. A comparison of the reliability of Pirsig's own motorbike with a companion's BMW becomes a gloss on the vagaries of existence itself. While the erotic suggestion of reciprocating engines alarmed the epicene John Ruskin, Pirsig saw in his flat-twin a suggestion of the divine.

The Truth About Motorbikes

Anybody who has attended to the maintenance of a motorbike knows this to be true. The great Italian designer Ettore Sottsass Jr once explained that the Japanese completely failed to understand the essential nature of the motorbike proposition. With the scrupulousness for which its civilisation is rightly admired, Japanese manufacturers built machines of a nearly flawless perfection, achieving astonishing levels of reliability. H-o-w-e-v-e-r, Sottsass continued, what bikers really want is a machine that demands attention. One that goes wrong and requires fiddly maintenance on an almost daily basis. The fun of owning a motorbike is to dismantle and reassemble its gearbox on the kitchen table.

Pirsig's intellectual successor was Matthew B. Crawford's *Shop Class to Soulcraft*, a surprise *New York Times* bestseller of 2010, a sentimental 'inquiry into the value of work' which lionised the philosophical comforts of artisan activity in the aftermath of the 2008 crash when draining a sump seemed a more important task than capitalising on the imbalance of markets . . . as it indeed is. To make the point, Crawford's book had a motorbike on the cover.

Pirsig was never quite clear, but his own inspiration was probably Eugen Herrigel's *Zen in the Art of Archery*, first published in German in 1948, but becoming something of a workshop manual for the Beats after its translation and American publication in 1953.

Herrigel had studied *kyuodo*, Japanese bowmanship. His subject was what's now known as the inner game: the belief that you can improve your aim by no longer thinking about your aim and letting automatic responses dominate consciousness. There's a mystical beauty there, but Pirsig was also advocating attention to detail.

To follow Pirsig's theory, transcendent perfection may also be experienced when sweeping the floor. And I think polishing mirrors would do just as well.

In the Zen tradition, sweeping the floor is often cited as a meditative task. Total engagement with something apparently trivial can be revelatory.

When Pirsig's *Zen* was reviewed in the stuffy *Times Literary Supplement*, the editors made what was for the title and the day a daring decision about the illustration. They chose a cutaway drawing of a Kawasaki motorbike, a rare intrusion of the technical culture into the literary environment. But, so far from Zen perfection, they chose the wrong bike: Pirsig's was, in fact, a 1966 Honda CB77F Superhawk.

Still, the choice of illustration once again showed how in the twentieth century industrial objects became elevated to the status of culture and supporters of literature and art. And, so far as Robert M. Pirsig was concerned, of philosophy and religion as well.

If you do not have a motorbike in need of replacement shims, you may have a dirty floor to sweep or a messy refrigerator which can be drafted in as a therapeutic alternative.

Mrs Thatcher once explained to me, as I am certain she had done to many others before, that one of the tasks she enjoyed most was cleaning the fridge. In the prime minister's busy life, where things did not always go well, or even near completion, cleaning the fridge was the rare example of an activity that could be begun and finished to total satisfaction in the course of a single evening.

Besides, fun to get to know the grommets, seals and hinges. Edit the mysterious unlabelled stuff long since forgotten in the freezer, edit the historic sell-bys, refresh the opaque ice cubes, polish the stainless steel. Polishing is usually good. Editing is always good. There are, for example, very few books that people wished were longer.

Deal with the pesky crumbs and shards of freeze-dried herb that have penetrated where the daylight never goes. And then give the whole thing a good buff with a stainless-steel treatment. I think it is entirely reasonable to take cleaning a fridge as an act that has very nearly metaphysical value.

Others found this to be true during The Great Isolation. A *New Yorker* cartoon showed a slightly confused-looking woman polishing a bathroom mirror and saying to herself, I guess I could spend all year doing this.

When I think of it, while cleaning the fridge might not engage the passions, it is, I suspect, probably more satisfying than chatting to Kim Kardashian in her orange rubber condom dress at the Met Gala. But that's mere speculation. And, anyway, she is probably busy planning her next Met Gala outfit. She'd be better off dealing with the fridge.

We have had that tempestuous season recently. Of course, it is not the business of economists to predict or manage global health crises, but it is notable how very flimsy and feeble and irrelevant economic theories appear in the context of what many thought might actually be the End of the World. **Given the prospect of oblivion, who would not prefer – in the brief moment between the crisis and the catastrophe – to consult *The Ode on a Grecian Urn* than the footnotes of the Heckscher-Ohlin Trade Theory.**

And yet, economists, exposed now as authorities with insights no more impressive than a voodoo witch doctor's, with theories in place of fetishes, continue to expostulate and patronise. Their explanation of behaviour merely makes sense of that behaviour . . . and that can lead to dizzying circularity in arguments. I'd hate to get caught in the trap of erroneous predictions – not least, because as the particle physicist Niels Bohr observed, predictions are very difficult, especially if they are about the future. But I am wondering if we may be hearing less from economists in years to come.

Inhaling the petrichor ever more deeply, it seems to me that at the same time as economists have shown what little value they can add, 'tech' has been revealed as not just the dominant but also the most melancholy influence in our lives. There's more to life than streaming police procedurals or next-day delivery.

Here's a simple truth: Californian computer entrepreneurs hijacked the term 'tech'. But technology involves lots of things besides computers and things that are a lot more interesting and a lot more useful: power generation, materials science, structures, transport systems, biomedical research . . . all of them more valuable and humane. And who were these tech entrepreneurs? Not a bunch of amiable zoned-out, sandal-wearing, alfalfa-munching, *I Ching*-reading hippies, world improvers with degrees from CalTech, but a mob of charmless, ruthless, dysfunctional, overly ambitious, money-grubbing, predatory sociopaths, entirely lacking in empathy or common sense. California's 'tech' has become at least as cynical as Detroit's automobile industry in the fifties. At least General Motors only corrupted your wallet.

What are now becoming known as California's surveillance industries have achieved something beyond the reach of even the wicked old Russian KGB and the sinister STASI, the East German Ministerium für Staatssicherheit, the Ministry for State Security. **At the height of its deranged imperium, the STASI had files on (a mere) 5.6 million DDR citizens. Facebook has 2.6 billion users. And the STASI needed to employ 90,000 spies to get that result. Facebook employs half that number**.

Facebook has spies who know what you are looking at online. Amazon's cameras track you around supermarket aisles, even if you would prefer that they did not. For all I know, the camera at the top of the screen of the MacBook Air on which I am typing this is sending real-time images of the face of a tormented writer directly to Cupertino or Menlo Park. Soon I may be scatter-bombed with ads for headache relief or creative counselling.

Someone, somewhere, is reading your e-mail, and if you leave the house with the help of Google Maps, you are being followed. Uber knows where you have been and could hold you to ransom if you are unwise enough to go places where you should not. They have files on you. But more than the KGB or STASI, whose goons simply reported what had happened, Facebook and Google can now *predict* your behaviour. That's if you let them. They used to say you have nothing to lose but your chains; workers of the world today have nothing to lose but their smartphones.

Once, profit came from the industrial processing of natural resources to make attractive consumer goods – that Cadillac described earlier. Whatever you may think of its crude abuse of the world's resources, the Caddy was a very innocent sort of pleasure for the consumer, and a very reliable source of profit for the manufacturer. It took you on a vacation for a while. Now profit comes from the electronic processing of curiosity and desire.

There is a good reason why this is a book not a Zoom call. Most importantly, I want these words to end up as a book because I think books are infinitely precious things. Moreover, a paper book remains the best-ever interactive data-retrieval system. And books do furnish a room.

Really, no one has advanced much on the achievements of Johannes Gensfleisch zur Laden zum Gutenberg, the European inventor of moveable type which made the mass production of books a possibility. (I say 'European' because it is very likely the Chinese had moveable type before Gutenberg's Bible of 1455.)

You can interpret someone's personality from a quick scrutiny of their bookshelves, not something you could do with a log of their Zoom calls. (Although Zoomers do, it appears, got to special trouble to arrange the books in the background so as to give a positive sense of scholarly propriety.) Plus, if you do not choose to use them as furniture, paper books are readily recyclable.

'People tell me that life's the thing, but – me – I prefer reading.'

Logan Pearsall Smith, *All Trivia* (1933)

But exactly why is Zoom so unsatisfactory? Since Cicero, sight has been considered the keenest sense. The anatomist Vesalius subjected everything to the 'authority of the eyes'. Modern neuroscience confirms these historical insights: perhaps 50 per cent of our cerebral energy is taken up by looking at things. And Zoom betrays that. As a medium, it does not facilitate communication; it frustrates it.

Zoom tech is so crude, distortions and delays are fundamental. In a Zoom call, people spend most time looking at themselves, and this loss of eye contact leads to a loss of trust. And people find Zoom encounters fatiguing because our finely evolved brains have become used to interpreting, often at a subconscious level, the little tics and breaths and eye movements and shrugs and fidgeting that are a normal part of any real human encounter. Smells too, of course.

And trying to compensate for this loss is tiring. The *New York Times* compared Zoom to processed foods, since interesting subtleties are smoothed and styled into a bland, if very jerky, format. And it said our brains work as 'prediction generators'. Not on Zoom they don't. Like processed foods, Zoom is not good for you.

And now I have suddenly acquired a rapidly developing fantasy about having a Zoom call with Mark Zuckerberg, the Facebook tyro, a high-functioning dork who has more influence on the future of the world than anybody who is not actually in possession of nuclear weapons or an army. Despite this awesome status, his critics see him as an emotionally stifled, morally confused, manipulative and predatory philistine. On the other hand, I am open-minded.

Mark Zuckerberg Q&A

Q: Mark, I want to tell you what I am wearing for this Zoom because I think it's significant. As you can see, I look like a Ralph Lauren tribute. Ancient, battered boat shoes. Faded pink cargo shorts and a pink polo with a popped collar for that old-school preppy look. I haven't shaved for three weeks. It's not a beard. It's 'not shaving'. There's an important difference.

A: Sure. [Rubs his smooth chin.] But I don't spend much time thinking about small things. I always wear a grey GAP T-shirt. I get through five a day. I throw them away rather than wash them. Makes sense.

Q: I have read that you only eat meat if you have killed the animal yourself. This sounds like an agreeable, if incongruous, sort of primitivism for Menlo Park. But I suppose it proves you have the pure instincts of a hunter-gatherer.

A: It's true that I have served dinner of lobster and goat I killed myself. But right now, I am on the Paleo diet. You know, seeds and berries. Hate to waste time on eating, man. But I'm cool with pistachios. According to the PDCAAS (Protein Digestibility Corrected Amino Acid Score), they contain all the nine essential amino acids. I'm into essentials.

Q: Good. That will include great paintings, then. When you're next in London, I'd like to take you to the Wallace Collection.

A: Sure, I'll send one of my local guys in an SUV to pick you up.

Q: Actually, I thought we'd walk from my place. We can go through several World Heritage sites on the way.

A: But my Cadillac Escalade has high-definition video, so we could visit the museum without getting out of the car.

Q: Thing is, I wanted to talk you through Nicolas Poussin's *Dance to the Music of Time*. You know, the allegorical painting about temporality that inspired Anthony Powell's famous sequence of novels. I think it's worth personal attention, because one's presence in front of an authentic masterpiece is a unique and transforming experience.

A: I'll get back to you on that. [Looks perplexed and consults his iPhone.] Sorry. Gotta call Xi Jinping.

Mastering the Curve
Why stuff matters

For nearly two centuries, people have been struggling for a definition of the word 'design', and no convincing one has been forthcoming. So, my own opinion has evolved that 'design' means having an aesthetic view of ordinary things.

Designers add value to ordinary stuff. The humble plastic bucket, for example. Even more on which below.

To a Marxist, 'design' means in their awful jargon **the commodification of surplus.** That's to say, the nefarious acquisitive processes of capitalism require demand to be stimulated by adding some sort of spurious value to manufactured goods.

In 1899, Thorstein Veblen published *The Theory of the Leisure Class*, one of the most influential books in what we now call 'sociology'. He took up this riff. To Veblen, ornament was a proud demonstration of wealth since it suggested the ability of those leisure classes to extract unnecessary labour from the working classes ... by paying for it. **Ornament was a ... status symbol.**

Veblen spoke twenty-six languages and is sometimes described, I hope incorrectly, as the last man who knew

Value

everything. He explained that in any society that rises above brutish subsistence, choices are made. The great art-historian Bernard Berenson put this in a nice and enduring aphorism: 'taste begins when appetite is satisfied'.

Of course, the word 'design' is older than the nineteenth century and came into English from the Italian '*disegno*', meaning 'drawing'. Italians also used the word '*ingegno*' to mean inventing. This never quite passed into English, although our word 'engineering' carries some of its freight.

But in both languages, the word 'design' acquired the additional meaning of intention. And something that is 'designed' *intends* to be better – which is to say more beautiful and more useful – than something that is not . . . although the fact that the design lobby has always claimed 'everything has been designed' makes a bit of a logical nonsense of this proposition. But nonsense has never bothered this tribe.

The essentials of 'design' itself remain as indefinable and mysterious as any creative activity. There really is no process which makes one object more 'designed' than any other. At some level, every artefact, sign and symbol was the process of a creative decision. And that applies to Fred Flintstone's arrow-heads as well as to Franz von Holzhausen's latest Tesla.

What designers do is bring an informed self-consciousness to making stuff. They have an aesthetic approach to the world, and it is this that fascinates. It is why designers are in the same territory as artists. I'd actually say that so far from design being a subset of art, paintings and sculptures are subsets of design.

Design in this version was about democratising luxury and aestheticising the ordinary: look upon that masterpiece plastic bucket and, please, take great pride in the achievements of our civilisation. 'Ordinary' is not at all the same as 'commonplace'.

The Museum of Modern Art/Scala, Florence

In 1957, New York's Museum of Modern Art recognised that a humble plastic bucket was worthy of display in its permanent collection. Two thousand years before, Socrates had recognized that a well-made bucket had aesthetic qualities.

Bucket? The fact that New York's Museum of Modern Art has a plastic bucket in its permanent collection does not strike me as risible, but as a triumphant defence of the analogue world and its values. This is Gino Colombini's KS1146 bucket designed for the Milanese firm Kartell in 1954 and acquired by MoMA three years later.

Socrates agreed.

Socrates on Design

When asked by Aristippus if a functional dung bucket could be beautiful, Socrates replied, 'Of course, and a golden shield ugly, if the one is well made for its work and the other badly.'

Designers often talk about finding solutions when really they are mostly stating old problems in a new way. But the world is losing its appetite for novelty, at least novelty of the desperate, neophiliac next-new-thing sort. We do not, for example, need another 'designer' chair. The 'problem' of the chair was solved long ago. No more experimentation is required. At least, not until new materials are discovered and human physiology has fundamentally changed. No one's anticipating either happening.

Follow this reasoning and it's soon apparent that the design sensibility moves from shaping products onto process and experience. And the biggest experience of all is life itself. The great distinguishing feature of modern life is that even as a bucket crept into a museum, aesthetics rushed through the gallery doors and out onto the street.

It is one of the distinguishing characteristics of the modern Italian world view that 'art' should not be separate from 'life'. This is why Italian manufactured goods are so often heartbreakingly evocative and beautiful, so often the very best of their type. Hence, the bucket.

Print editors know that a cover of a book or a magazine showing, say, a 1963 bright-red Fiat 1500 cabrio with Naples plates driven by a Gina Lollobrigida wearing Persol sunnies and a Pucci sundress will attract unusual attention in bookstalls and newsstands.

And this Fiat was not, technically speaking, even a notably good product; it just looks wonderful because it was designed and built by artisans whose skills can be traced directly back to shield-beating Etruscan metalworkers. It suggests a *continuity*, even as the little Fiat also suggests a nagging doubt that great beauty exists only in the past.

But if they excel at everyday beauty, an appreciation of everyday delight is not a wholly Italian prerogative. A reverence for machines is a defining characteristic of the classic design sensibility. I have two superlative and treasured examples from mad Germans. In 1910, Joseph-August Lux published his book *Ingenieur-Aesthetik* where he argues 'the technical and stylistic achievements of modern times are revealed most clearly in contemporary machines'. He illustrates his belief in the chapter 'A Bicycle Is Beautiful'.

And a bicycle *is* beautiful: there is little that is superfluous, and you can read it as a fascinating graphic of dynamic forces. Bicycles are also very efficient, and, in one way or another, efficiency often leads to aesthetic (as well as to practical) elegance.

His countryman Curt Ewald agreed but was more concerned with boilers than with pedals. Writing in the influential magazine *Die Form* in 1927, Ewald gave us all his thoughts on the shape of railway locomotives. Here, with eyes prepared to look, the pistons, boilers and bogies are the 'actualisation of a plan . . . through the most perfect, simple and economically appropriate means'.

Pained commuters on Thameslink or Metro-North Railroad or Paris's RER may squirm, but one of the great accomplishments of the twentieth century was to establish the idea that real aesthetic value could be found in things as ordinary as bicycles and trains.

Another truth about design – and this is a notion that includes the Arts and Crafts of William Morris, the Swedish House Beautiful movement, the German Werkbund and the Deutsche Industrie Normen (DIN), the Bauhaus, Jazz Age chrome flash, Detroit Kitsch, the Italian postwar Ricostruzione, minimalism, streamlining, the museum-and-morality-inspired Gute Form and 'Good' design campaigns, ironic postmodernism and almost any other style label you care to mention – is that it was the last gasp of the analogue, material world, a world of *aesthetics*, before digital infatuation took over and virtual impressions trounced the weight and texture of old-fashioned solid stuff.

The belief that technology refined by art could create democratised beauty was one of the great persuasions of the twentieth-century design movement. With the perspective of the twenty-first century, we can, however, now see that the idea of 'design' itself was also a persuasive myth, although a benign one.

Like all mythologies, the design movement threw up some god-like figures whose job was to sustain the belief system. The idea of the designer as a shaman, as a wizard – perhaps even a divine consultant – who can create beauty where hitherto there had only been mess and squalor had no better champion than Raymond Loewy, who set up the first independent industrial design practice in New York in 1927.

He was no moralist, and many find him a vulgarian, but Loewy never felt much need to apologise for either failing. If that is what they were.

I met him on several occasions in both London and New York, so I know. He was vain, superior, immaculate, tanned, perfumed (he used to splash Chanel No. 5 into his scuba suit to take away the smell of rubber), proud, intolerant, lacking in empathy and absolutely fascinating.

Raymond Loewy Q&A

Q. So what is design?

A. Good design keeps the user happy, the manufacturer in the black and the aesthete unoffended.

Q. What's your motto?

A. Never leave well enough alone.

Q. What is the place of beauty in modern life?

A. Between two products equal in price, function and quality, the better-looking one will outsell the other. I can claim to have made the daily life of the twentieth century more beautiful.

There was never a better example of what it was to be a designer, even if much of his work, by the lights of the twenty-first century, makes the squeamish flinch.

Loewy is presented here not as any sort of moral exemplar (he was, to add to the descriptors above, a tad shifty and possibly unscrupulous as well), nor even as a specially accomplished designer (his taste was grotesque), but as an individual who fully understood the potential of his moment and his place in it. You would not call him 'mindful', but he was most certainly rooted in the here and now.

A French émigré once described as an inch deep and a mile wide, Loewy practised modern witchcraft: he cast spells on ugliness, turning ugly ducklings into beautiful swans.

In the middle of a startling and very well-publicised career of charlatan-like legerdemain, repairing the ugly products of industry by dressing them with his own thoughts, Loewy wrote a very good book. Or perhaps had a very good book written for him. *Never Leave Well Enough Alone* was published in New York in 1951.

When an edition appeared in his native French, it was retitled *La laideur se vend mal* (ugliness does not sell), but the theme was essentially the same. Namely, ugliness does not sell, because there is a popular preference for beauty, even if beauty is exasperatingly difficult to define.

We'll soon question that proposition, but with impressive chutzpah, lashings of chrome and eau de cologne, and a gaudy sense of style, Loewy turned misbegotten industrial products into soothingly beautiful ones. And trousered fortunes in doing so. He told his blinking clients that the most beautiful thing in the world was a rising sales chart.

He translated the awkward and the banal into the elegant and fetching. He even described the early days of the Machine Age as 'messy dirty noisy bulky' and famously streamlined into sleek perfection a hitherto messy, dirty, noisy and bulky Pennsylvania Railroad locomotive. These ugly characteristics could, by his improving genius, be eliminated. This gave us the model for what 'design' could do, at least in its first version. He made hissing steam and filthy soot and hot metal *aesthetic*.

Design was the avenging angel, remedying ills. *Never Leave Well Enough Alone* has a series of transformations from ugly to beautiful: the Gestetner duplicator, the Coldspot fridge, Flexvac vacuum-seal packing machines, Coke dispensers, the International Harvester cream separator, the Cummins cheque-perforating machine, the Singer vacuum cleaner and the Mobil car battery.

If you can make office equipment beautiful, why ever would you not?

So, here was the remedial power of design to turn ugly mistakes into beautiful purpose. This was the alchemy of design! To beautify! To tidy up! To exclude dirt! And, by the way, to sell. To create commercial and cultural value . . . through industrial aesthetics.

And this was good.

Loewy's style was a world away from the pristine reductivism of the Bauhaus and its followers, even if he had opened his New York studio in 1927 when the Dessau Bauhaus was just one year old.

While Loewy did bravura sketches of speedboats from his Palm Springs rancho-deluxe or his plush Park Avenue apartment with Chinese lacquer and carpets to drown in, more earnest designer–penitents, men such as Wilhelm Wagenfeld and Max Bill, made fastidiously reductivist designs for clocks and glassware which won the approval of the Museum of Modern Art (if not, to be honest, of much of the public).

Eventually, the 'design' of the twentieth century will be seen as a discreet art-historical period, as nearly precise as baroque or rococo. It had its masters, its disciples, its beliefs, techniques, disciplines, debates and critics. The synoptic history of recent art (which is yet to be written) will explain that design awareness was exactly the same sensibility, a shared aesthetic, as Marcel Duchamp's sly conceptual outrages which often involved misappropriated machine or tools demonstrated. He was a provocateur and controversialist of unique genius. But his example marks the beginning of the moment when artists began to abandon beauty. Or perhaps when beauty began to abandon art.

Duchamp's argument was persuasive: mass-produced urinal or snow shovel were art because he said so. Follow this reasoning and value might be found in a plumber's merchant or a hardware store, the artist suggested. He gave erotic heft to a coffee mill. At about the same time, a dim US Customs official attempted to slap an import tax on a Constantin Brâncuşi sculpture because he felt the sleek metal casting was probably a piece of industrial or medical equipment and not an abstract *objet de vertu*.

Quite soon, Loewy, Duchamp and Brâncuşi will be seen with Max Bill and Wilhelm Wagenfeld, industrial designers of the severest German school, not as very different personalities, but as witnesses to an identical phenomenon: the elevation of the everyday to the status of art.

There were three high-water marks of this infatuation with the mechanical. In 1934, New York's Museum of Modern Art put on its *Machine Art* exhibition, and the poster showed a roller bearing in dramatic chiaroscuro, the light-and-dark presentational technique of Caravaggio. Of course, the only intention of the roller-bearing manufacturer was to offer a device to reduce friction in a mechanical assembly.

Then, in 1951, MoMA's Philip Johnson curated an exhibition about cars – a world first in a museum context – which he memorably described as 'rolling sculpture'.

Then, in 1957, there was the beatification of Colombini's brightly coloured plastic bucket. In the way that the Catholic Church occasionally canonised its heretics to defuse their power, the outrage of Duchamp had been normalised by the gift of the label 'good' design.

The word 'good' is always a treacherous descriptor, but the belief in 'good' design was Holy Writ for a certain influential lobby. While any disinterested view of history shows that tastes change, often risibly so, it was an article of faith that good design not only has an aesthetic character, but lasts for ever, transcending time. This may very well be fallacious, philosophically speaking, but bringing beauty and eternal values out of the museums and galleries seems to me a very good thing.

Yet it's become fashionable for leading architects to disdain beauty, just as 'fine' artists abandoned the pursuit of it long ago.

If Raymond Loewy with his flamboyant and curvaceous material hoopla, his flash 'n' cash, can stand for the analogue age, then Mediated Matter Group of the auspicious Massachusetts Institute of Technology can stand for the uneasy world of twenty-first-century design and its struggle for relevance in the virtual moment.

The Mediated Matter Group champions the idea that finding and understanding new materials will lead to new creative possibilities. The architect's tools are no longer a Rotring pen and a drawing board. His materials no longer lumps of masonry and girders of COR-TEN steel. His tools no longer a trowel, a hammer and a crane. The architect is a wizard who deals with computational abstractions and finds, at least if he belongs to MIT's MMG, inspiration in silkworms, oyster shells and human breath. This is some way from 1934 when the Museum of Modern Art felt it quite correct to put an SKF roller bearing or a ship's propeller on display near Picasso. Mediated matter was, and some may see this as a portent, the subject of a MoMA exhibition in 2020 . . . access to which was compromised by emergency regulations.

Elsewhere in MoMA, not far away from the plastic bucket is the 1957 Braun Kuchemaschine, a food mixer designed by

Dieter Rams that will stand as an everlasting expression of German Gute Form: austere, rational, beautiful, very much analogue. Its politeness and formal perfection now make it look as alien to us as the august circumcision rites of the Bukusa people of Kenya.

Platonic Problems/Cookie Dough

'The problem with taking Platonic perfection into the kitchen is that it gets dirty.'

Reyner Banham in conversation

Neri Oxman, a fashion-conscious spokeswoman for the Mediated Matter Group, married to a Wall Street Titan and rumoured to be romantically involved with Brad Pitt, explains how the new sensibility is suspicious of beauty: 'When artificial life can be created in vitro, mastering the curve ain't enough.'

Of course, it is not wrong to suggest that the design sensibility can advance from the mere shaping of things towards a more cerebral shaping of process. But it's surely wrong to dismiss physical form. Loewy's streamlined fridge and Rams' food mixer might be things of the past, but for so long as we have senses of sight and touch, they will be important reference points for beauty.

Despite the disdain of mediated materialists, mastery and appreciation of curves remains a priority for aesthetes . . . and that today means everyone. At least until we have evolved into a species so sophisticated that physical pleasures are dispensable, and we plug our electrodes into the ventral tegmental area of our brains and swoon in a collapse of artificially induced dopamine overload.

And so long as humans want to make judgements about things, there are good plastic buckets and bad ones. I know this because I have asked Alice, our cleaner. She has user-generated insight here.

The valuable thing is to make a determination about the curves of buckets. 'I don't care about plastic buckets' is not a valid response, since the denial contains a confession of the opposite. A denunciation of anything simply serves to show how very seriously you take it.

A generation or so ago, Nicholas Negroponte of MIT's Media Lab, patron of the Mediated Matter Group, made visionary statements about the digital future. But he had some difficulty in promoting his cause: a crusade for the digital age and all the imagined opportunities and liberations it would bring. His *Being Digital* of 1995 was a fine argument for the imminent virtual nirvana, but he had to use forestry products and ink to make his case.

Similarly, the Mediated Matter Group had to use an analogue exhibition to set out its stall. This was called *Material Ecology* and was scheduled for MoMA before The Great Isolation shuttered the museum. Maybe, with hindsight, it was tempting fate, in a crisis involving aerosol droplets of a deadly virus, to put on a show about giving form to breath.

Of course, new attitudes to and new horizons for the design mentality to explore will always be detected. The creative urge is a fugitive one and not susceptible to orderly behaviour. But for so long as humans have responses to touch, sight and sound (smell and taste beg different arguments, since they are cerebral while the former are more tactile), there will be a continuing need for tangible objects. Beauty too.

Steve Jobs of Apple said you know a design is good if you want to lick it. That was intentionally provocative and salacious. But it was also good evidence for the continuing importance (and value) of physical sensations. You cannot have a digital lick.

And it is a beguiling paradox that the supreme artefact of the digital age, Jobs's iPhone, was a meticulous work of craft: as sleek a conduit as you would ever want to traffic internet sewage. Significantly, the iPhone's designer was taught by his silversmith father a proper respect for materials and how to work them. He says that in his workshop he takes aluminium to the limit and in so doing new forms present themselves. Understanding exactly how you can bind glass to metal creates unique character. The iPhone is beautiful.

And, as Raymond Loewy had maintained: ugliness does not sell. Thus, the iPhone has been an outrageous commercial success, making its $2-trillion manufacturer the wealthiest company in the world. That, if you like, is the value of design. It can, among other things, buy you an impressive cash pile.

This designer was Jony Ive, but while his understanding of design very much involves a state of mind – 'putting an unusual amount of care and effort into things' is the way he describes it – it is also about unalloyed beauty.

German Pedagogy and the iPhone

There is a direct line from the prewar Bauhaus in Dessau to the Hochschule für Gestaltung of the fifties in Ulm to the iPhone that is completely ubiquitous. And that line was drawn by the food-mixer designer Dieter Rams (1932–). With the delightful air of a benign mad professor, Rams gave physical form to the spirit of the Wirtschaftswunder in his splendidly stripped-back products for the Brain electrical company: from the 'Snow White's Coffin' record player of the sixties to the black boxes of the eighties. I interviewed him once at his office in Kronberg im Taunus. He winningly explained that it was good to use grey in interiors because it allowed the colours of nature to sing out. Then he pointed to some white tulips. Rams' aesthetic was fully adopted and cleverly adapted by Jony Ive of Apple.

No matter how effective it is as a tool, a large part of the iPhone's success can be attributed to its uniquely lovely form. Its aesthetic values are as lucid and disciplined as a classical painting by Nicolas Poussin ... the one I wanted to show Mark Zuckerberg.

'My nature constrains me to seek and love well-ordered things, and to flee confusion which is as much my antithesis as light is to dark.'

Nicolas Poussin (1594–1665)

In painting, Poussin's is the ultimate classical proposition: controlled yet powerfully moving . . . for those with the patience to read it. Or to read that bucket.

It's always worth remembering what makes a classic. The great literary critic Charles Augustin Sainte-Beuve said a classic is both universal and permanent.

And that's exactly what great design aspires to be.

The Contadino Effect
How to be a peasant

'Wherever you are, you find the sun, a blade of grass, the spirals of a dragon-fly. Courage consists of staying at home, close to nature, which could not care less about our disasters. Each grain of dust contains the soul of something marvellous.'

Joan Miró, *Cahiers d'Art* (1936)

These are strange – but inspiring – days, when sardines are a more sophisticated choice than smoked salmon. And they will likely be served on a rough-hewn plank, not fine china.

In these strange days, cosmopolitan cooks choose a pasta called *grano darso*, one made of burnt wheat husks, a form of agricultural waste that is almost worthless and has a mouthfeel approximating to that of scorched carpet felt. These husks were once fed to pigs. In these strange days, a difficult sour and cloudy 'organic' wine *is* preferred to an aristocratic 'Super Tuscan'.

A simple life is not a reduced life. On the contrary, the taste for simplicity acknowledges the fascinating complexity of things. Keeping things simple enhances

rather than diminishes the scope for enjoyment. That charred sardine? If you concentrate, it's probably more truly satisfying than a complicated *plateau de fruits de mer*.

In these strange days, to declare 'I want to be a peasant' is to become vulnerable to a charge of ambitious elitism, of claiming unearned privileges. The peasant was close to nature, an enviable position to occupy . . . at least as seen from the perspective of a frazzled urbanite. Any fool can lead a busy life today. It takes art and application to find simplicity. And that is where real value is to be found.

But rediscovering peasant values does not, unless you wish to do so, involve wearing felt leggings, living in a wattle-and-daub hut with a mud floor, shared with cattle, a mule and pigs, while having a life expectancy of thirty-five on a diet of mush and thistle stems.

Peasant Life: A Reading List

Gerald Brenan *South from Granada* (1957). A Bloomsbury-ite recovers from the noise and the people of the First World War in a *pueblo blanco* in the Alpujarras.

Anton Chekhov *Peasants* (1897). A novella with a grimly realistic view of rural life.

John Clare *Poems Descriptive of Rural Life* (1820). Lyrics by a Suffolk poet–peasant.

Elizabeth Luard *European Peasant Cookery – The Rich Tradition* (1986). An encyclopaedic account of *bas cuisine*.

The Great Isolation tipped a lot of people into an awareness that something mysterious and indefinable has been lost when we all have forty-eight-inch HD televisions and smartphones with computing power to rival the Pentagon of the Vietnam era, when Uber fetches us hither and yon, when Deliveroo brings us a dinner we could not make ourselves following a sequence of clicks and the transmission of however many billions of electrons it takes to turn desire into a Wiener schnitzel brought to you by a man on a bike.

Brillat-Savarin

The great gastronome Jean Anthelme Brillat-Savarin's unforgettable observation in *Physiologie du Goût* (1825) was 'tell me what you eat and I will tell you what you are'. To which we might today add: tell me where you like going to eat, and I will tell you what you are trying to be.

I actually heard someone say, without evident irony, that 'Camilla loves her micro herbs. And she'd go an awfully long way for a miniature carrot.' Maybe Camilla would, but Camilla is also wearing a silly Prada hat. Meanwhile, our peasant wants herbs that are robust and carrots the size of your forearm. Our peasant wants to eat for survival and satisfaction, not to decorate or impress.

During the Great Isolation, it was notably amusing to see with what glee the media reported that as traffic froze in North Wales, goats came down from the mountains and started wandering the newly quiet streets of Llandudno. How very close people suddenly felt to ancient pastoral and bucolic mythology. Wild boar were seen in Marseille *centre-ville*.

And in this perplexed mood, there were sensible voices advocating the reintroduction of the wolf into a United

Kingdom that has been without the benefit of the presence of *Canis lupus* since the fourteenth century. This was something hitherto discussed only by cultists or fantasy-fiction writers of the second rank.

Rewilding is now a conceptual, if not yet large-scale, reality. What else is Stefano Boeri's 2014 Bosco Verticale in Milan but an emphatic architectural polemic about how we need some sort of concord with nature? It is a seventy-six-metre apartment block drenched in vegetation: about eight hundred trees of twenty-three different species. It's a green tower that's a welcome punctuation mark in the too often arid narrative of modern cityscape. It would be misleading to call the Bosco

Molteni Motta/Getty Images

Stefano Boeri's Bosco Verticale was finished in Milan in 2014. Why travel to the country when the country can come to the city?

Verticale an architectural manifesto for the uncomplicated peasant sensibility, but it is certainly evidence of a new reverence and respect for nature.

The old peasant mentality might have been founded in a rude struggle for existence. The new peasant mentality is about identifying and indulging in habits of lasting value. And to a great degree these habits centre on food. As, of course, does life itself. True, with our sardine on its rough-hewn plank we are gentrifying the peasant aesthetic, but the practice of gentrification depends on the conviction that there is something essentially attractive that can be improved, if not actually bettered.

The Leonard Cohen character in Polly Samson's 2020 novel *A Theatre for Dreamers* says, 'When there is food on the table, when the candles are lit, when you wash the dishes together, and put the child to bed together, that is order, that is spiritual order, there is no other.'

Seeds of this awareness were sown nearly forty years ago, and, of course, the agricultural image suggested by 'seed' is entirely appropriate. In 1986, Elizabeth Luard wrote a monumental study of European peasant food and made us excited by writing 'hanks of tripe', or discussing the trapping and skinning of rabbits, or the social conduct of the piggery. Blood pudding? Now you're talking. Who wants pallid refinement when you can have heroic blood and guts?

This awareness lurched forward when in the same year as Luard's book a radical journalist called Carlo Petrini founded the Slow Food Movement in Piedmont. His first act of agitprop was to organise a demonstration against the opening of a McDonald's near the Spanish Steps in Rome, something he felt to be sacrilegious in a city where spinal cord of ox or *animelli di vitello* were staples of the traditional diet. Ronald McDonald was not welcome in the city of the Popes and Fellini. The only thing a Roman wants deep fried is an artichoke in the Jewish style, those famous *carciofi all giudia,* not a patty made from salvaged beef or an industrial French fry.

But maybe the absence of French fries in Italian life has had its effect. A later act of agitprop by Petrini was to steal the chips off my plate during a lunch at The Wolseley while he explained that 'only two things are necessary for the continuation of human life. And they are sex and food. Each is best done slowly.' And then he ruminated over another purloined French fry.

Time – or at least speed – means less to a peasant than it does to a burger flipper. Or mechanical time does. True, peasant life necessarily acknowledges the rising and the setting of the sun. And, of course, the imperative of the annual harvest cannot be ignored if your life depends on turnips. But your peasant is not a card-punching clock-watcher.

Middle-class Italians, including bankers from Milan, some of them perhaps already living in the Bosco Verticale, found themselves wanting to become a Lucchesian or Puglian or Campanian *contadino*, swapping a Canali suit for overalls and a Lamborghini Gallardo for a Lamborghini Spike Trend open-field tractor.

Yet I have seen how a *contadino* really lives. Never mind that a real *contadino* lives in semi-squalor with a flickering colour TV on top of a chest-freezer and drives an unwashed Fiat Panda. The real *contadino* may well eat frozen food, and of the Tuscan idyll, with its *l'andana* of cypresses, he cares nothing. His is a hardscrabble existence which he would likely swap for shelf stacking in Conad. He lives in dirty clothes and has a limp.

The Chapman Corrective

In 1935, the pioneer cultural anthropologist Charlotte Gower Chapman travelled to rural Sicily to observe the lives of peasants. Her account – published as *Milocca: A Sicilian Village* in 1978 – is a nice corrective to the idyllic view of Italian rural life presented by, say, *Condé Nast Traveller*. The landscape is yellow, harsh and broken with outcrops of gypsum, not the fine cultivated greenery of Tuscany. Houses have livestock (and, occasionally, the elder son) on the ground floor, with living accommodation above, accessed by an external stair. There are probably no windows and no formal chimney, just a hole in the roof of red pan tiles laid on cane. In winter, heat is provided by burning almond husks in a copper pan while the family huddles around in shawls. This family eats from a common platter and drinks from a common glass. Flour is ground as needed and the sign of the cross is made over bread. In the fields at lunchtime, the man of the house may eat a raw artichoke or a bunch of grapes.

But we have said that these are strange times. The appeal of an imaginary peasant way of life was not so much prehistoric as post-technological. Agencies have appeared with names like Jobincountry or AgriJob. The *New York Times* reported, 'Until recently a return to the land seemed reserved for natural wine hipsters or gentry sowing boutique gardens with ancient seeds.' Now it was an elemental pull.

Developing a peasant sensibility is a process in fact requiring great sophistication.

The classic definition of peasant culture comes from Robert Redfield's *Peasant Society and Culture*, the standard work on the subject from 1956. This is a culture where farming is 'a livelihood and a way of life, not a business for profit'. Thus, the newly minted peasant instinct is to return to the land and the locality and to the unarguable logic of the seasons with their different weathers and crops and their daily confrontation with eternal truths.

So, the *contadino* effect is the exact opposite of globalisation and faceless industrial agriculture: almost the entire US market for meat is served by only *four* enormous processing companies. You do not need to be an unemployed Milanese banker scared of the Plague to want to find a better way of providing food than the meatpackers Tyson of Springdale, Arkansas. They are the ones with the chlorinated chicken. Our *contadino* wants his *pollo* in the wild, not in chemicals.

Bandwidth and download speeds and obscure financial instruments suddenly seemed less interesting than lots of dishes cooked in *umido* or *al forno*, with lots of *pasta fritta, crostini di pollo* and recipes like *panzanella* which actually demand stale bread. What a liberation from globalised (which is to say Americanised) norms of industrial food, with its fake freshness and sell-by dates, when *stale* bread actually becomes a desired ingredient. Or *garmugia*, a one-pot thick soup that looks like cattle feed. Moreover, the limitations of the peasant's single pot are stimulating, especially if that pot is impressively carbonised.

Unfortunately, the *New York Times* had to report that many of the ex-urbs who sought new and meaningful work through AgriJob turned out to be useless at working on the land. Moroccan immigrants, whether they had papers or not, were much preferred.

To John Ruskin, cookery meant English thoroughness, French art and Arabian hospitality. And it required intelligent knowledge of fruits, herbs, balms and spices. To Ruskin, Italian food counted for little, but the intrinsic values of Italian food seem especially meaningful today. Much more so than the absurd refinements of the Michelin stellar system, with its polished sauces and rising cloches. The more sophisticated you are today, the more likely you are to demand peasant food, not a dish requiring five litres of veal stock. Eventually, even the haughty Frenchmen recognised that people don't want swooshes of purée, blobs of jus, ziggurats of foam or any other fetish of hoity-toity cheffery: in 2021, it was decided not to publish the *Michelin Guide Rouge* for the United States.

Adieu, then, Paris and Roanne, Eugénie-les-Bains and Saulieu. *Buongiorno*, the Val d'Orcia. 'The world of the Italians,' Marcella Hazan, the most influential Italian food writer in American history, writes, 'is not a phenomenon that needs to be subdued, reshaped, arranged in logical patterns . . . It is not a challenge to be won. It is there simply to be enjoyed.'

Best of all, Italian food represents a 'serene relationship between man and the sources of his existence'. Yes. We need more of that. It has sometimes been said that if a certain type of French food shows off the genius of the chef, too often a very look-at-me genius, then Italian food shows off the genius of God. And in an historic moment when people are hungry for values, this quasi-religious character is the gravamen. Italian food has no artifice. No correction. No manipulation. And, at the same time, the simplicity of Italian food makes it the most accessible of all world cuisines to the home cook.

During The Great Isolation, there was a remarkable rise of interest in bread-making. In the United States, there were reports of thin women in immaculate, deluxe gym wear from

LuluLemon, including tights that had never felt sweat, manhandling fifty-pound bags of specialist Italian 00 flour onto powered industrial trolleys to raise their farinaceous loot onto the load-deck of their glistening SUVs. During The Great Isolation, the first thing British supermarkets ran out of was . . . flour. A nation of shopkeepers became a nation of bakers.

Making dough for bread became, for many unpractised cooks, a form of therapy. And the more peasant-like was the sourdough, the more therapeutic the effect. Some ambitious souls began building pizza ovens in London gardens so the spirit of Locorotondo or Palermo could be kindled at home. People took a new interest in herbs and their effects. I know one individual who once relied on *grande marque* champagnes as reliable aphrodisiacs beginning to consult Nostradamus and preparing his herbal concoctions to replace the fizz.

In England, we lost our peasants before any other country, hence our own yearnings for the values peasant life appears to offer are correspondingly more intense. The reason people go on holiday to Tuscany and Dordogne, or anywhere intensely rural, is that the basic systems of existence are unavoidable and gratifying. These we have lost but are now keen to recover.

Illogically, but emotionally, an expensive holiday in a Tuscan villa or a Perigourdine *maison de maître* offers rapid access to a primitive way of life long lost at home. I would not say that visiting Carrefour connects you with cosmic time, but going to the supermarket defines the day. The French are the only people who attach a cash value to flavour. *Cherchez le pain!* (And in this context, it is irresistible to mention that 'praline' is slang for 'clitoris', proving a fine connection between food and pleasure in French culture.)

> ## Holidays
>
> It was not always Tuscany or the Dordogne. *Murray's Handbooks for Travellers* were created for a Victorian middle class, newly acquiring a taste for travel because of the railways. The sequence of their publication is revealing:
>
> 1830s: Holland, Belgium, Prussia, North Germany, Rhineland, Denmark, Norway, Sweden, Austria, Tyrol.
>
> 1840s: Egypt, Greece, Turkey, Italy.
>
> 1850s: Spain, Portugal.

And, while not eating, what else might you do when a peasant? Sweeping a polished stone floor in bare feet with quiet reverence and throwing away the woeful Dyson might be two things. In any case, the Dyson never worked properly in the first place. And it's true that air-dried laundry is softer. How precious is that smell of freshly mown grass?

Best Broom

The best broom has, since 1998, been made in glass-fibre reinforced air-moulded polypropylene by Magis. The designer is Stefano Giovannoni. This is a tool so beautiful it is never hidden in cupboards but often left on display as a stimulus to contemplation. In use, it has a pleasantly calming effect on the user.

And our deluxe peasant villa will be filled with 'Higher Junk' – tablecloths, crockery, cheese safes, rusted iron whisks, blunt knives with bone handles – artfully sourced from the local *brocante* or occasional *grenier-vide* or the Sunday market in Panzano in Chianti, now famous not for great art but for the presence of a celebrity butcher. This is the way values are headed.

This visual mood was beautifully caught in the metaphysical still lifes of the Bologna painter Giorgio Morandi. If you want to find enduring value in calmness and domesticity, meditate on a Morandi painting where jugs and glasses and crocks are treated with the reverence once accorded to archangels. Better still, replicate Morandi effects at home.

The Art of the Lemon
Fruit can make you happy

Let's consider the lemon. Lemons can help. Can there be anything that more quickly connects us to a rural idyll than the sight of this fruit? Henri Matisse reckoned oranges were all you needed to know about heaven on earth, but I think he underestimated the lemon.

A lemon has simultaneous suggestions of freshness, goodness and exoticism. (Although, strange to say, it is that strange fruit whose flesh is rarely eaten, its skin and zest being considered more valuable.)

Top Tip

Lemon zest is a marvellous accompaniment to sea salt on twice-cooked chips.

And a Splendid Recipe

Tagliolini alle scorzetta di arancia e limone. This is from Helena Attlee, whose *The Land Where Lemons Grow* (2014) is a masterpiece of (agri)cultural history. Blanch thinly cut peel of two oranges and one lemon. Set aside. Cook chopped onions very gently in butter, adding white wine, cream and the juice of the fruits when the onions are translucent. Cook down a little, having added the blanched peel, then use it to dress the *tagliolini* (although any pasta will do). Salt and pepper to be deployed, obviously.

I have brought a lemon to my writing desk as inspiration. Specifically, I have brought a *limone femminello sfusato amalfitano*, the type that arrived in southern Italy from the Middle East in the tenth century.

Willem Claeszoon Heda – PHAS/ Getty Images

Banished in rural Yorkshire, Sidney Smith described his plight as being 'ten miles from a lemon'. From the Jewish tradition on, lemons have been regarded as sacred. And an inexpensive source of great beauty.

In the kitchen, we have a huge white porcelain dish of them. There is nothing which raises the spirits more and less expensively. I have lemons as my computer desktop. The sight of a lemon invites you on a journey. At first cultural, then sensorial, lastly gastronomic. There is value in a lemon.

Lemons are sacred in Judaism. Jewish exiles found them in Babylon and took them home in 539BC. Different types of lemon are sacred to different Hebraic tribes, and all tribes use lemons in the rituals of Sukkot.

The Medici collected lemons and prized certain examples as more valuable on account of their deformities, rather than despite them. The *limonaia* is a status symbol that's a remembrance of this. 'Nature made private' was how Francis Bacon described it in the seventeenth century.

Lemons were once so precious that at a banquet organised by the Company of Leathersellers for Henry VIII and Anne Boleyn at Westminster Hall in 1533, a single lemon was given pride of place above the capons, swan and sturgeon. My Amalfi lemon costs about 95p, but its effect is way more valuable than caviar.

When he was sent to a living in rural Yorkshire (where he described the countryside as a 'healthy grave'), Sydney Smith all alone bemoaned his outcast state by saying he was 'ten miles from a lemon'. This was a condition of nearly intolerable disadvantage, since it suggested a distance from civilisation, as well as a limit on appetite.

Pound sterling for pound weight, a lemon is the most value you can find. Probably even better than the potato we began with. And with one on your desk, you can pretend to be in touch with a *contadino* from the province of Salerno.

To me, that's a good thing.

Thoroughbred Lemons

Sfusato amalfitano is southern Italy's outstanding lemon variety, at its best for a mere twenty days, its short span adding to its mystique and allure. Amalfi Lemon Experience (www.amalfilemonexperience.it) organises tours of its lemon-growing terrace one kilometre above this dramatic coastal city.

Coffee Maketh the Heart Lightsome
Ceremony and ritual in the kitchen

There *are* domestic gods, and it's a good idea to practise propitiation of them. Propitiation being another term for 'ingratiation'. If there are gods, you don't want them riled.

The Romans believed in them, and I see no reason why we should not. At this stage, I'm not sure whether the gods travelled with me to this house, rather like divine pilot fish, and made their home here too, or whether they were already resident in the property and made my acquaintance in due course. Whatever, they are everywhere, but ours, I feel certain, tend to cluster in the kitchen near where we keep the spare blades for the MagiMix.

Why here? Because the kitchen lends itself to rituals. And gods are suckers for them. Since eating is an unavoidable daily necessity, its refinement may as well become a thoughtful ritual. Making coffee with a certain stylish solemnity can, for example, turn ordinary routine into lasting pleasure.

To write this section in the middle of the afternoon on a sunny day, I have (somewhat reluctantly) settled into my study with my notes and a very good cup of instant coffee. You have

coffee if it is too early for wine. (Although you can always add
a splash of brandy to the espresso to make *caffe correto*. This can,
as many Italians will testify, be drunk at any time of day and is
especially good in the morning.)

There are degrees of excellence in instant coffee and
only someone completely perverted by snobbery would not
acknowledge that. Some instant coffees do, indeed, resem-
ble dusty floor sweepings and taste as bitter as burnt tar.
But choose a good-quality Freetrade decaf and you have a
quality drink. In any case, the best instant coffee is not technically very distinct from a really finely ground 'delayed'
coffee. And, as always, technique and attention to detail are
important.

The taste will be directly affected by the amount of granules
and the ratio they are in to the water, which should be very
hot but not boiling. And, if at all possible, the water should be
filtered and not emerge from a tap in an opaque liquid stream
which, if you are in London, also contains significant elements
of oestrogen and cocaine residue. Water that has been drunk
before. And I should have mentioned that I do not actually use
a cup, something which seems a false refinement for a drink of
this sort. I use a chunky Duralex glass, an all but unbreakable
classic of vernacular design that would have been just as at
home on Lenin's or Le Corbusier's writing table as it is on mine.
I like that thought.

Really, only a fool could not make and enjoy decent coffee
made from granules and presented in a way appropriate to its
style. Nonetheless, there is a requirement for selection, care-
fulness, inventiveness and watchfulness. Thus, making even
instant coffee rivals dinner in its ritual significance.

But after the frivolity of instant, on to the even more serious matter of delayed coffee. After the shower with quality soap, making coffee is the second important ritual of the day. Although in history coffee has often been seen as a beverage which grants social promotion on its consumer, tea being either effete or proletarian, it is for most of us an essential to start the day. (But ideally only after a *canarino*, hot water with a slice of lemon: a 'canary to clear the system'.)

The coffee revolution of recent years has created new levels of value and meaning. While once there was no choice, now there is very nearly an embarrassment of it. Thirty years ago, even in central London, I had to drive five miles to find proper coffee. Now there is scarcely a city street anywhere in the country without a vendor of skinny chai latte with a triple shot. As I say, new value has been created where none had existed before. **Our imaginative vistas have been extended by baristas.**

When I was a teenager, the arrival in Liverpool of a coffee bar called El Cabala suggested that Merseyside was making tentative steps towards cosmopolitan sophistication, something not yet wholly realised. Certainly, I took it that way. I adored the menu as much as I adored the Italianate Slim Jim tie I wore while mulling it. Cappuccino, the El Cabala proprietors' menu told me, was so-called because it was inspired by 'the coffee-coloured habits' of the Capucin monks. I felt there was a nice ambiguity there.

And the bar's name suggested the agreeably esoteric practices of the Kabbalah, just as the fizzing and spluttering and chromium-plated Gaggia machine suggested High European *modernismo*. To this day, I associate finely frothed milk with avant-garde design. I did not know then that Pope Clement VIII called it 'Satan's drink'.

And, despite or because of its Satanic associations, in history coffee became first subversive then avant-garde: Balzac drank fifty cups a day (even if ten milligrams of caffeine in less than four hours can be fatal). He called it '*le carburant des grandes artistes*' (the fuel of great artists) and said it roasted his guts, although he did not explain why this was a good thing. And with its long traditions, this fuel of the great artists lends itself to pleasing rituals in its preparation.

The Arabic word *qahweh* was first a poetic term for wine but was diverted from the grape and towards the berry. Of course, no true record of coffee's origin exists, but the familiar legend is that an Abyssinian goatherd noticed more liveliness in his animals when they had been chewing the coffee plant, and this effect he sought to replicate in himself.

At first, the beans were crushed in goat fat, an option the normally inventive Starbucks has not yet added to its menu. Only in the thirteenth century of the Christian era did it occur to anybody to *roast* coffee beans, grind them and infuse the powder in hot water. In this form, *qahweh* was popularised in the Levant by whirling dervishes who found its stimulant properties useful in maintaining the alertness required during their ferocious and exhausting head-spinning dances.

Soon, coffee became part of domestic rituals in Islamic homes. It should, according to an old Arab saying, be **prepared with art and drunk with art.** Houses were designed around a coffee room, and the ritual went beyond the mere roasting, grinding and infusion to become a social event.

There was, when drinking coffee, a repertoire of well-practised greetings and gestures, compulsory praise of Allah for his munificence, polite enquiries into everyone's health and, with an African servant assisting, guests would be served in an order that very clearly indicated the status hierarchy.

'[Coffee has] . . . many excellent virtues, closes the orifice of the stomach, fortifies the heart within, helpeth Digestion, quickeneth the spirits, maketh the heart lightsome, is good against Eyesores, coughs or colds, Rhumes, Consumption, Head-Ache, Dropsie, Gout, Scurvy, King's Evil and many others.'

A London newspaper advertisement of 1657

So, it's reasonable to take this coffee ritual very seriously. Additionally, it takes me on an imaginary journey to places with exceptional coffee traditions, places where kitchen gods cluster in force. Possibly to Gilli in Florence, possibly to the Bar Canova in Rome's Piazza del Popolo, which the great Fellini used as an informal office, or possibly to James Joyce's Trieste, which is Italy's coffee capital.

Here, in Vienna-on-Sea, the coffee entrepreneur Ernesto Illy (who had a doctorate in the synthesisation of morphine) established with impressive didacticism exactly how to make the perfect espresso. Illy is the Ferrari of coffee. The water, he said, should be between ninety and ninety-five degrees Celsius. The beans should have been roasted at precisely 220 degrees and exactly fifty of them are needed for a single dose of twenty-five to thirty millilitres of *espresso*.

Espresso actually means 'squeezed'. Expressed at a pressure of nine atmospheres, espresso should be drunk when its temperature is not less than eighty degrees. As in the Arab world, in Trieste milk and sugar are considered contaminants. Meanwhile, the quality of the espresso may be judged by the density of the *crema*, which provides both a medium through which the coffee is imbibed but also traps the flavoursome essential oils.

So, there is a lot to think of every morning. And that's even before any decision is made about what method to use to make the coffee, if not an electro-mechanical high-pressure espresso: a French drip? A cafetière (or what the Americans call a 'French press')? The *machinetta napoletana*, a Bialetti Moka, a Turkish *ibrik* or a simple china jug?

These decisions all add value to the ritual which, no matter how often repeated, remains an everyday mystery that is continuously pleasurable. And in the morning, for me, always in that tiny Duralex glass. Always preheated with very hot water. This detail is critically important.

Voltaire thought coffee was 'slow poison', and I reply, 'Very likely, but what's the hurry?' Meanwhile, T.S. Eliot's miserable J. Alfred Prufrock in his eponymous 'Love Song' measured out his dreary life in coffee spoons.

And the critics cannot agree whether this meant Prufrock was looking back in sadness or anticipating the future with dread. Pondering the 'decisions and revisions which a minute will reverse', Prufrock finds the coffee ritual confirms the banality of his existence.

'I have measured out my life with coffee spoons;
I know the voices dying with a dying fall
Beneath the music from a farther room.
So how should I presume?'

> T.S. Eliot, 'The Love Song of
> J. Alfred Prufrock' (1915)

But my own coffee ritual is life-enhancing for the reasons sketched above; it engages me with a richly satisfying cultural history. And it is doubly life-enhancing because I start the day with carefully prepared coffee and ... a vicarious reading of the latest obituaries, which is even more life-enhancing.

'What people do with food is an act that reveals how they construe the world.'

> Marcella Hazan, *The Classic Italian Cookbook* (1973)

Good to start the day propitiating the domestic gods, but a similar ritualistic attention can be applied to any kitchen routine – vinaigrette, for example. This should be made with all the ceremony of a pagan Basque priest officiating at the cult of the god Mari. Although, if you prefer, you can buy bottled oleaginous filth in a supermarket.

You can judge anybody's moral credibility by the quality of her or his vinaigrette.

The valuable assumption is that every meal following the morning coffee ritual should be theatre, not a mere intake of nutrients. And since wine succeeds coffee in the course of the

Value

day, you could mainline alcohol and it would give you a buzz, but enjoying the subtleties, complexities, associations and wonderful *taste* of wine is a superior experience, since higher faculties are involved. And higher faculties should be engaged every day.

How to Be a Wine Taster

Pour a glass.

(Remind yourself that four things alone describe any wine: the grape, where it is made, the craft of the maker and the year of its making.)

Is it red or white? Or what?

Sniff the still liquid. What are the primary aromas?

Swirl the liquid. What are the secondary aromas?

Look at it. Does the liquid have clarity?

Drink. Is the taste sensation long or short?

And what does it remind me of?

Do I like it?

Take notes on every new bottle.

There really is not much more to it.

Anyway, *vinaigrette*. Do you reach for the bottle of ready-made supermarket glop dense with E numbers and polluted by aberrant dried herbs or elect to engage in a satisfying form of manual labour which if done well, taking care in the selection of the correct ingredients and treating them with respect, will demonstrate that you are a highly evolved human being? Making vinaigrette is a test of character as well as a test of taste. It's not a mere emulsion; it's evidence. Devotion, skill and materials are on display and being tested.

The same can be said of risotto. Making it is a matter of reflection, not of urgency. It is something not to be hurried. Apparently simple, risotto requires discrimination and effort, patience and concentration too. You cannot take your eyes off the pot, nor let your stirring arm relax. It is a matter of the infinitely slow addition of stock to the lightly fried rice. Then you stir and you stir and you stir until the starches break down and the mixture becomes an unctuous gloop. You can add cream to simulate the process, but that would be cheating.

Perfect Vinaigrette

The problems with vinaigrette are usually too much vinegar, bad oil and . . . not enough sugar. This last is an outlaw addition but – measured correctly – can ensure approval. The classic mixture is one part vinegar to four parts oil. And, of course, it must be the best wine vinegar. Not brewed industrial condiment. You must first dissolve the salt and sugar in the vinegar, since they are not soluble in oil. Garlic, if used, must be pounded to a smooth purée. Mustard and black pepper are acceptable additives. Elizabeth David has in her *Provincial French Cooking* (1960) a recipe for '*sauce vinaigrette à l'oeuf*' with chopped shallots and chives, with a boiled egg yolk beaten into the emulsion and chopped white added at the end.

Bad Trips
Home versus abroad

After The Great Isolation, there were questions raised about whether you need bother to travel the planet's surface when you had already arrived at home. The questions went both ways. People discovered the peculiar satisfaction of domesticity, but enforced confinement also stimulated an almost demented wanderlust.

There *are* reasons to travel, but perhaps fewer than there once were.

There are 195 countries on Earth. I have been to perhaps thirty of them. And of one thing I am certain: there are fewer than thirty countries to which I care to return.

Yet they say the urge to travel is instinctive. It's rooted, perhaps, in a racial memory of our knuckle-dragging simian ancestors schlepping across the savannah in pursuit of comforts and pleasures they found unavailable at their last resting place.

Brighter destinations over the rainbow are so fixed an element in literature that the taste for them may be instinctive. Aphra Behn was perhaps the very first English novelist, and she introduced her readers to an agreeably exotic dream world which has ever since been one of the major preoccupations of literary writers.

I specially enjoy the opening sentence of Rose Macaulay's *Towers of Trebizond,* a novel of 1956. It's a classic of its sort: '"Take my camel, dear," said my Aunt Dot, as she climbed down from this animal on her return from High Mass.'

In *Oroonoko,* which was published in 1688, Behn described, for example, the 'inconceivable wonders' of Surinam. Inconceivable indeed for anyone who had actually been there. The all too conceivable *horrors* of Surinam included dengue and yellow fevers, hepatitis, typhus, a wide variety of water- and vector-borne diseases, malaria, and protozoal diarrhoea. But reality has a weak hand when compared with the value of a dream world . . . the more inaccessible, the more powerful the urge to experience (or even just to imagine) them.

During The Great Isolation, thinking about travel went two ways. One direction was taken by a group maddened by the privations of working from home, curfews, compulsory distancing, sheltering in place and inflamed with a restless lust for new destinations, or even just the rediscovery of favourite old ones.

Another group found it just fine staying at home.

The business case for recreational travel is founded on the idea that cultural assets have a value that can be exploited for gain by the organiser. The cultural case for recreational travel is founded on the idea that the experience is an edifying one.

And while it was the Grand Tourists of the eighteenth century who defined . . . *tourism,* maybe the larger idea of tourism was founded on something rather older. An instinct for moving about and for discovery may indeed be a fundamental human attribute, driven by that need our ancestors felt to find new territories to exploit. Never mind the club-wielding ancestors on the savannah or the steppe, the transhumance, the seasonal migrations of sheep and shepherds (still a reality in the Mediterranean) might be seen as a historic prototype for the seasonal crowds arriving at Gatwick North Terminal already wearing sombreros.

But cultures risen above subsistence find other reasons for travel: curiosity and a civilised taste for leisure and pleasure. A wealthy Roman of two thousand years past might have his *villa marittima* on the coast at Ostia. A Renaissance pope might have his summer palace in the hills of Frascati.

And the English? They have always searched for better weather and more art.

The Grand Tour was an eighteenth-century gap year, a rite of passage, an initiation ceremony. 'Every blockhead does that,' James Banks declared of the Grand Tour and then, confirming the allure of travel, instead went to the South Pacific to observe the transit of Venus with Captain James Cook and, duly, more or less discovered Australia.

No other European aristocracy attached so much significance to European travel as the English. And its history is wonderfully telling about how enduring values can be and, indeed, how they can evolve.

Carrozzeria Touring

To illustrate the influence of the Grand Tour in Italy itself, look no farther than the designer of James Bond's Aston Martin: Carrozzeria Touring of Milan. The English word 'touring' was chosen in 1926 to indicate the sophistication of this traditional 'coachbuilder'. Additionally, it was Italian manufacturers who coined the term 'GT' for a style of fast, luxurious hard-top sportscar. 'GT' stands for 'gran turismo', which is, of course, Italian for 'Grand Tour'.

The expression 'Grand Tour' makes its first appearance in the language in Richard Lassels' travel book *Voyage of Italy*, which was published in 1670. Although here the Grand Tour refers to the necessary transit of France. Quite correctly, Lassels says that once in Italy it is a '*Giro*'.

But to the Grand Tourists, France was really a distraction. They were not even much interested in the palaces of Versailles or Fontainebleau, although pleasures were to be had in Paris: here the *milordi* would stop to buy bright clothes and do a little anticipatory whoring to establish a rhythm. But Italy was always the dedicated focus. Only here could young unsophisticated Englishmen be polished into a serviceable version of humanity.

But first you had to cross the Alps. While today the pleasures of mountain scenery are a given, once upon a time little value was found in mountains. In fact, mountains were thought repulsive. When the diarist John Evelyn crossed the Simplon in 1646 . . . he was nearly speechlessly horrified.

But by the time the Grand Tourists had helped establish recreational travel as a civilised ideal, the view of mountains, at least metaphorically, had changed. Lord Tennyson could stand on the spiky, Gothic roof of the Duomo in Milan, stare at distant Monte Rosa and go into a proto-psychedelic rapture. A little later, the biographer Leslie Stephen spoke of his feeling for mountains as a form of idolatry. He was ready to prostrate himself before 'these gigantic masses'. Stephen was Virginia Woolf's father, and who knew he was a practising mountaineer?

The greatest value and prestige were to be found in more southerly parts of Italy. In his great Dictionary, Dr Johnson said a man who has not been to Italy 'is always conscious of an inferiority'. He even suggested that the very purpose of travel was to see the Mediterranean . . . and then go beyond. And D.H. Lawrence (probably thinking of wet English Sunday afternoons in Nottinghamshire) gloomily said the Englishman only feels comfortable travelling south.

The Grand Tour declined as an institution at the end of the eighteenth century. First, because Napoleon's territorial adventures presented practical difficulties for the traveller. Second, because the railway soon made it a more democratic activity. Then, travel became commodified, so less value was attached to the experience.

The Package Tour

The first travel agent was London's Cox & King's, founded in 1758. Modern travel was very much an invention of the newly industrialised English, evidenced by the existence of hotels called 'Bristol' everywhere from Beirut to Thessaloniki to Paris. The source seems to have been the well-travelled 4th Earl of Bristol, the Bishop of Derry, who had a well-developed taste for luxury. Later, the Carlton Hotel in Cannes and the Promenade des Anglais in Nice also reveal English influence.

Mass tourism may be said to have begun in 1841 when a messianic Baptist called Thomas Cook organised a return trip from Leicester to Loughborough for members of the Temperance Society. By 1855, Cook's abstemious tourists were in Paris. Then, the world.

Thomas Cook Archive

The first packaged holiday was a tour organized by Thomas Cook: in 1841 he chartered a train to travel from Leicester to Loughborough.

The distinction between the Grand Tourists and the first Package Tourists can be seen in the art of their respective days. To the Grand Tourists, it was the meticulously realistic paintings of Canaletto, which accurately recorded the surface, that appealed. But to the Victorians who knew photography, J.M.W. Turner's luminous canvases better presented the mystery and the magic of abroad.

But it seems almost impossible to demystify Italy, to rob it of an allure still felt powerfully today (despite, like Surinam in the seventeenth century, modern Italy having many disagreeable aspects).

No one caught the yearning better than W.H. Auden in his 1958 poem 'Goodbye to the Mezzogiorno':

> Out of a gothic North, the pallid children
> Of a potato, beer-or-whisky
> Guilt culture, we behave like our fathers and come
> Southward into a sunburnt otherwise.

Sightseeing
Why do the wrong people travel?

First, there had been the disruptions of Napoleon's adventures which closed Europe to travellers. Then the railways and Package Tourists put an end to the glory of the Grand Tourists as democratic arrangements succeeded aristocratic ones. But the legacy of the Grand Tourists was sightseeing: that rare thing both free and priceless.

And there never was a more committed sightseer than the art historian Bernard Berenson. His diaries record an almost erotic relationship with buildings; it was a sense of rapture. You cannot be in a building such as Rome's Santa Maria Maggiore, Berenson believed, without having your standards and values enhanced.

In Rome, on 2 November 1947, he writes, 'Loafed about in Santa Maria Maggiore enjoying the gorgeous space of the nave, the perspective of the columns, the splendour of the great chapels.' He was indefatigable in his looking. A physically frail, bird-like man, he could cheerfully spend all day in punishing Roman heat, inexhaustibly curious about everything:

ruins, monuments, pavements, every bust, every relief, every oil painting, every fresco, every moulding.

His visual appetite was voracious. He had patience, precision and apprehension. He loved to wander. And he recognised that being in the presence of great art had an effect on him that was not always conscious. There was a mystical connection between his person and the art. He had the fervour of a pilgrim, the energy of a sportsman and the curiosity of an explorer.

And his diary notes are beautifully precise. On 20 June 1954, when a very old man, he rose early and was on his hotel's 'balcony between 4:15 and 4:45, flat quiet light, mother-of-pearl tone with touches here and there of rose in the sky. Water oily, seemed to be flowing in but drift went the other way.'

These fine words **turn a view into a masterpiece.** And that's something we might all do . . . with practice.

The year before, again very early, this time dawn on 24 May 1953, Berenson observed Etna from his balcony in Taormina:

Its colour was silver and mauve over a gentle glow from within. A diadem of snow and below a necklace of cloud. The height of the mountain reduced by its long slopes. The sea mirror reflecting and at the same time intensifying the colours of the sky and the sky itself blushing, flushing with the sunlight coming from below and making itself felt, although not yet visible to the eye. A calm with no sound but the muted one of the sea breaking as it reached the shore.

See what value there can be in calm, but precise, observation.

A Very Different Writer Has a More Facetious View of Volcanic Effects

'I do not think I shall ever forget the sight of Etna at sunset, the mountain almost invisible in a blur of pastel grey, glowing on the top and then repeating its shape as though reflected in a wisp of smoke, with the whole horizon behind radiant with pink light, fading gently into a grey pastel sky. Nothing I have ever seen in Art or Nature was quite so revolting.'

Evelyn Waugh, *Labels* (1930)

For the benefit of society, it should not be forgotten that even before The Great Isolation forced a practical re-evaluation of travel options, a view was forming that recreational travel may soon be a thing of the past. At least, a view was forming amongst the sophisticated that this might be the case. It was becoming *le monde à l'envers*. Once, rich people were fat. Now, rich people are thin. Once, only the rich could travel. Now, the rich may prefer to stay at home. The old assumptions were changing even before The Great Isolation.

Just as the best sex is above the collar, not below the belt, the best travel is often in the mind. The great journeys are often internal ones. For the fastidious, there is an argument that travel does not broaden the mind, it narrows it.

The conquest of space was, before it became a preoccupation of the Kosmicheskaya SSSR and NASA, a nineteenth-century preoccupation. First, the railways conquered space and time. In the twentieth century, the automobile and the plane continued the process. In the twenty-first century, electrons have supplanted boilers and pistons and turbines as agents of conquest.

Meanwhile, after a long debauch, we may have exited the age of frictionless, endless, brainless travel. Post-viral, flying to Prague for £9.99 for a piss-up with the boys on Friday night becomes very clearly the obscenity it always was.

Tourist Versus Traveller (Tentative Definitions)

The French novelist and traveller Marie-Henri Beyle (whose nom de plume was 'Stendhal') coined the word 'tourist' to describe an individual with a refined eye for beauty, a person who travelled for pleasure.

But that was then.

The modern tourists are not demanding of anything other than unlimited cheap booze. They prefer collective activities and lack both independent spirit and intellectual curiosity. Tourists participate in a destructive farce that, absurdly, destroys the value of the places they choose to visit.

Travellers are the opposite of the above. They make their own itineraries. They avoid crowds and seek out the unusual in gastronomy. Travellers respect the dignity of their destinations.

Then there is the 'tripper', a lower category still.

I once took part in a Conservative Party Conference debate about low-cost air travel. I'm a libertarian–hedonist free marketeer, but my argument against it was based on environmental concerns (not just carbon but also contrails, the condensation of which is at least as damaging as soot because it alloys as clouds, which, in their insulating effect, increase global warming), plus a growing anxiety about destinations being destroyed by what Italian officials call the *maleducati* ... tourists who are not intellectual descendants of the Grand Tourists. Tourists who drop McDonald's Styrofoam boxes in the Piazza di Spagna and run burger grease on Michelangelo. Against this, I advocated self-denial, restraint and social responsibility.

Against me was the delightful Simon Calder, a traditional socialist – not just in ideology, but in his sandals-and-socks costume too. But here again was *le monde à l'envers*. Calder argued in favour of free markets, consumer choice and the price factor. He advocated unreflective self-indulgence. I was concerned with principles. He was concerned with convenience. Of course, in front of an audience who depended on EasyJet to get value from their golf-and-cocktails timeshare in Marbella, I lost.

The belief that travel is necessarily a private pleasure or a business necessity is one of the great delusions of our age. Henry Ford's gasoline buggy was intended to facilitate escape from the boredom of life on the farm. Now, the liberating machine is oppressive. Besides, boredom has its value, as we will later see.

By about 2010, it was already evident, research showed, that young people preferred a smartphone to a car. Their mobility had become virtual, not based on explosive propulsion with flammable liquids. When I was twenty, I was free because I had a car. My children now feel free because they do not.

Anyone who has spent time in an airport lounge can sense

how utterly nugatory most 'business' travel is. Rheumy and dyspeptic lost souls assembling for a jet to Frankfurt at five in the morning with only a muffin for comfort are not an edifying sight.

Meanwhile #1, study the anxious, doleful faces of leisure travellers at any airport and ask yourself if the activity involved is beneficial. An airport lounge reminds me of Kierkegaard's comments about birth cries and death rattles. Who could expect to enjoy what's in between?

Meanwhile #2, London's Crossrail will be completed at just the moment when commuting is finally exposed as a ludicrous proposition. 'Working from home' was once a euphemism for 'unemployed' but has become a perfectly reasonable proposition. Often enjoyable, too.

Alas I am not a poet, but for a long time I have had an opening couplet nagging me to become one. It goes 'The places I will never go/The list gets longer every day'. I can hear the as yet unwritten rhythms in my mind's ear, and the theme is absolutely clear: the bitter-sweet mixture of promise and disappointment, delight and dismay that is forever part of travel's baggage.

In this reading, tourism is destructive. And that applies to home as well as abroad.

John Ruskin's orotund Biblical cadences boomed around the nineteenth century, echoing off many monumental *and* celebrated causes. At just the moment the great railway stations were being built, he sensed the impending horrors that would come from high-volume travel.

In a preface to Robert Somervell's *A Protest Against the Extension of the Railways in the Lake District* (1876), Ruskin wrote a classic of rhetorical invective. It is also perfect evidence of his hatred of 'the stupid herds of modern tourists', as well as evidence of his need to save the same stupid herds from descent into hellish ugliness as they debauched their destinations, as the bus loads in Florence and the cruise ships in Venice do today.

Ruskin was concerned by the new railway running from Windermere to Keswick. He complained of 'the frenzy of avarice' which was the culture of its conception and execution. His favourite landscapes were to be blasted into a treeless waste of ashes. Sheep, he said, will be driven from Helvellyn. All of Wales and Cumberland will soon be blown up into a heap of slate shingle. And in the course of this ludicrous process, noble Grasmere will become a cesspit and its beach a bitter landscape of broken ginger-beer bottles. All this simply to find minerals and slate that offers only to roof all of England into 'one vast Bedlam'.

The Educational Benefits of Rail Travel

'What the new railway has to do is to shovel those who have come to Keswick to Windermere – and to shovel those who have come to Windermere to Keswick.'

John Ruskin, in Robert Somervell's *A Protest Against the Extension of the Railways in the Lake District* (1876)

What Italians call the *maleducati* is a polite way of saying 'low value', which is a polite way of saying 'poor'.

Sensitive visitors to Rome or Florence are now as likely to be impressed by brainless crowds, litter and filth as by great art. To be frank, in a competition for attention, litter and filth win. Venice has ignored every innovation except the tourism that's destroying it faster than the rising waters of the lagoon.

What we need to rediscover is . . . exaltation.

So exalted was Stendhal's own response to the wonders of Florence that he described himself literally fainting at the stimulation of all the sightseeing. This state of collapse is now known as Stendhal's Syndrome, a coinage by an Italian psychiatrist in 1979.

Petite Mort

French *intellos* can become overexcited by aesthetic experiences. Roland Barthes found reading so ravishing that he described his response to a good book as '*petite mort*'. This 'little death' originally meant 'fainting fit', perhaps a little like Stendhal's Syndrome. But it has come to mean the dazed rapture of orgasm. This benign state of aesthetically inspired ecstasy-collapse remains a valuable possibility, if one not always easy to realise.

Time to redefine it. **They say travel broadens the mind. But perhaps the opposite is truer.**

Flight has been drained of enchantment. The jet plane promised to democratise the luxury of air travel, but instead it universalised mediocrity, spreading suburbanism across the planet. Globalisation means Americanisation. And Americanisation does not mean Manhattanisation; it means everywhere gets to look like Des Moines.

Noël Coward was once asked about his flight and replied that technically it was a great success, but socially

left quite a lot to be desired. Why not have competitive entrance exams testing air travellers to world cities for acceptable levels of taste and decorum?

All transport systems combine the genius and folly of the human imagination and lard that with absurdity: fantastic machines used for banal purposes. Ask any traffic jam. Most modern cars will obey voice commands while en route to Sainsbury's. A generation ago, that was sci-fi. Or stand on any street corner in a deadbeat town and look at the cars go by. What strange, melancholic vistas are these glum travellers considering?

The answer is that all recreational travel is founded on the belief that authentic gratification exists somewhere else. Travel is about desire, which is to say: yearnings played out over time and space, wants projected into the future. (Business travel is based on similarly unreliable delusions about prosperity unattainable at home; when 'unnecessary' business travel was halted in Gulf War 1.0, there was no evident effect on the global economy.)

Clearly, cultivating desire is a valuable activity. Desire is the essence of, for example, car design, whose very origins are based on fantasies about travel. First, Henry Ford's promise that he would deliver his customers not so much to a destination as deliver him from the evil of crushing tedium. Vistas of escape! How they torment us.

If you have a well-organised life, leaving home for a gruesome airport or a characterless car will mean a reduction in standard of living. And this applies to railways as well.

I recently passed through Paris's Gare de Bercy, the dark side of the City of Light. Here was cruel mockery of the romance of travel. Here, in a litter of Heineken tins, was that *monde à l'envers*: once, the privileged classes travelled continuously; now it is the dispossessed. Paris's Gare du Nord consequently resembles a *pissoir* rather than a portal to romantic destinies.

Rich people used to have a lot of luggage. Now they have none. The amount of baggage carried through an airport is a reverse indicator of prosperity.

In any case, the more sophisticated you are, the less you move about. Crossrail, Google's driverless car and HS2 are not the start of something new but the end of something old. Like Concorde.

And these were thoughts that were all current and viable long before The Great Isolation made them almost compulsory.

'Why do the wrong people travel/When the right people stay back at home?'

Noël Coward (1962)

Even before a medical emergency made it prudent to stay at home, the advantages of refined domesticity were becoming very nearly obvious. A great remedy for insomnia is to have an internal list of people who are having a worse night than you. And a great remedy for the unscratchable itch of wanderlust is to know some fine anecdotes about horrible journeys.

Apsley Cherry-Garrard's *The Worst Journey in the World* is a classic of this genre. It is his 1922 account of Robert Falcon Scott's disastrous Antarctic expedition. Few people ever had worse nights. But personally, the apotropaic genre I like best is the one written by women travellers. These will teach you that staying at home has its benefits. Returning to England in an uncomfortable Channel storm in 1718, Lady Mary Wortley Montagu thought her wanderlust had been cured:

> I think the honest English squire more happy who verily believes the Greek wines less delicious than the March beer, that the African fruits have not so fine a flavour as golden pippins, that the *becafiguas* [the fig-pecker] of Italy are not so well tasted as a rump of beef; and that, in short, there is no enjoyment of this life out of England.

Of course, you can argue it both ways.

Gourmet Bathing
False economy and real value

Money, it's agreed, has its limitations.

Money can't buy you love. But it can buy you soap.

Buy the best soap you can afford. I can't really put it much more simply. However, it might be even better advice to buy soap that it is way beyond your budget. I don't believe anyone has ever been censured for smelling nice and having good skin tone. The hell with the expense.

Although if more reasons are required for luxury soap, here's a favourite Spanish expression: '*el caro es el mas barato*' – the most expensive is usually the cheapest. The Italians say this too: '*chi piu spende meno spende*' – he who spends most, spends least. Perhaps it is significant that the English, with their ineradicable residue of Puritanism, have no precise equivalent.

We perhaps say 'false economy', but that seems less poetic than the Spanish or Italian. 'False economy' sounds aridly technical and thin-lipped and disapproving, but the Spanish and Italian expressions suggest an entirely joyful and indulgent philosophy. I suppose another English expression of approximate equivalence is 'cheap and nasty'. The suggestion being, if you are going to spend any money at all, you need a better criterion than a low price.

The soap argument continues in this way. You probably wash every day, so make it a pleasurable indulgence, not a chore. What would be the arguments against? There are no known civilised alternatives to systematic hygienic practices, so why not make a shower or a bath into a ritual performance and, as has been said, to hell with the expense?

With soap, you can spread a little popular well-being through perfume and a generous spirit. Who is not affected by bergamot and laughter? While the dynamics of attraction – probably – transcend offensive odours, few friends have actually been won because someone smells like an old trainer. Besides, why not enjoy yourself? And why not enjoy yourself every day? Possibly with bergamot and laughter.

And there is the additional anticipatory pleasure of first choosing the soap and, eventually, unwrapping it with ceremony. If you are in the right mood, it can be a process tinged with a whiff of eros as well as *melograno* or vetiver. Manufacturers know this and spend a disproportionate amount of money on packaging their soaps.

And don't let this soap degenerate into a disgusting slither of decomposing chemical glop, a handful of slippery Proterozoic slime. Throw it away while it still has firmness, character and scent. This, you will find, is valuable advice.

It is quite difficult to think of a culture where having a bath does not have a profound metaphysical significance, since purification rites of one sort or another are central to civilisation.

But, of course, there is the pleasurable aspect as well.

There really are very few things more wonderful than a glass of very cold champagne in a sepulchral and warm candle-lit bathroom. Of course, you will already have excellent soap. Candles, as Thoreau knew, illuminate darkness while electricity destroys it.

Henry David Thoreau

Henry David Thoreau (1817–1862) pioneered cabin porn when he went to live in his primitive hut in the woods of Walden, Massachusetts. His time was spent, mostly, in close observation of nature. Was he an inspired romantic or a misanthropic, peevish scrooge?

The reference point for all valuable sacraments is the Japanese *cha-no-yu*, the famous tea ceremony. Here is a simple ritual elevated to the altitudinous levels of High Art.

Bridgeman Images

Cha-no-yu is the Japanese tea ceremony, a ritual taken to the highest degree of refinement. Japanese culture attaches similar significance to appreciating incense and flower-arranging.

'The art of tea is the aestheticism of primitive simplicity' according to Daisetz Suzuki, the great populariser of Zen in the twentieth century. This is a beautiful thought, but also a slightly delusional one, because the tea ceremony protocols are, in fact, highly sophisticated and complicated, a result of a frequently rehearsed formality practised over centuries.

What do I mean? In the standard work on traditional Japanese architecture, Edward S. Morse's *Japanese Homes and their Surroundings* of 1886, it takes an entire densely printed page simply to list all the items and accessories necessary for the proper enactment of this ritual which is quintessential to Zen. To reach the desired state of harmony, purity and tranquillity, an enormous amount of kit and philosophical prep are required.

And you will need a room about ten feet by ten feet, preferably in a pine forest, to perform your *cha-no-yu*. This room should be serenely simple. The tea appears first in the form of a very finely ground powder. A brush made of three eagle feathers is mandatory to clean the edge of the fire vessel. One Victorian observer found it 'uselessly absurd' but was nonetheless transfixed. Uselessness has its value.

And the tea ceremony influenced all the Japanese arts, but especially the ceramics that were essential to it. Interestingly, in a psychological context that aims at spiritual flawlessness, a tolerance for wear and tear in the crockery became a part of the mystery of the ritual. An affectation of roughness and of poverty was already present in the design of *cha-no-yu* equipment, but if a ceramic vessel became accidentally damaged, it would be repaired. And this repair would be in a technique known as *kintsugi*: a lacquer-like medium would be blended with gold dust so that a repair was not disguised but emphatically visible.

Zen aims to outmanoeuvre the intellect, to transcend time. However, *kintsugi* has a poignancy because it acknowledges the frailty of stuff and how stuff might be altered in time. Yet the presence of repair hints at the possibility of eternity.

Whatever, the respect paid to a mere plate reveals a culture which attaches mystical value to the presence and condition of things. The suggestion is that your plate has a meaningful life of its own that can be usefully extended, perhaps indefinitely, by diligent repair . . . rather than being contumaciously discarded after being cracked.

This is all closely related to *wabi-sabi*, the aesthetic that makes a virtue of imperfections, an aesthetic that accepts the inevitability of decay and finds beauty in it. A translation of the term is almost impossible, but the great populariser of *wabi-sabi* was a Californian counter-culture artist called Leonard Koren – a one-time resident of the fabulous hippy community of Point Reyes Station – who once wrote a book about the best techniques to rake leaves and published a magazine called *WET: The Magazine of Gourmet Bathing*.

Koren explained that *wabi-sabi* is a 'nature-based aesthetic paradigm that restored a measure of sanity and proportion to the art of living'. *Wabi* suggests the spiritual inner life, while *sabi* suggests external form. Basically, the doctrine is that beauty exists in the inconspicuous, and Koren, who had lived in Japan, makes the nice point that just as modernism revolted against the grossness of Victoriana in Europe, so *wabi-sabi* was Japan's departure from the overwrought gorgeousness of much inherited Chinese art and design.

Another fine explanation of this highly nuanced aesthetic is a short meditation by the novelist Junichiro Tanazaki. *In Praise of Shadows* was published in Japanese in 1933 and in English forty-four years later. It is an invitation to investigate the dark, where other senses might be more acute. Hence, the appeal of a cool breeze on the face in the darkness or the sound of rainwater dripping from a gutter. Chapters include 'On paper, tin and dirt' and 'Beauty in the dark'.

In observing shadows, Tanazaki found evidence of the beauty of impermanence: if anything is fugitive, it's a damn shadow! He argues that while the West values clarity and explication, the Japanese prefer complexity and subtlety. Specially, they enjoy the enigmatic interplay between the transitory and the eternal: nothing is ever perfect, but nor is anything ever finished.

There is surely compelling informal evidence that Japanese brain chemistry must be decisively different to ours, since they have developed a uniquely subtle apprehension of the world, finding value where no one had expected to find it. In gutters, roughness, rain, decay and dirt, for example. The same Japanese who have the fanaticism to develop carbon-fibre propeller shafts for a Subaru WRX (a component which will never actually be seen) also find enduring pleasure in the contemplation of a broken pot or a rotting plank or the way lichen forms on stone.

How to Be a Zen-inspired Aesthete

Decide on whether you prefer to be a grubby Italian *contadino* or a meticulously groomed Japanese *bonze*.

Meanwhile, stay calm.

Prepare to accept beauty in a variety of forms, sometimes surprising ones.

Tolerate damage and decay. Enjoy them, even.

Take delight in nuance and uncertainty.

Do what you can to manage a fulminating ego.

Respect even the most banal routines: elevate them to the status of ritual and perform them with scrupulous thoroughness and with dignity.

Try to put the Satan of mechanical time behind you.

Disdain neophilia: a taste for novelty is not sophisticated.

Realise that putting your socks on can achieve the grace of the *cha-no-yu*, given the right attitude and the best socks.

Do not complain about going grey: the passage of time ordinarily makes people and things more valuable and more beautiful.

The other role of the shadow, besides stimulating contemplation in Zen adepts, is to tell the time. The sundial is one of the most ancient of inventions and one touchingly suggestive of man's fragile grasp of existence. 'Adam,' Charles Lamb said, 'could scarcely have missed it in Paradise.'

Perhaps not, but the passage of the sun, and therefore the implied passing of time, was presumably first noticed by one of the Flintstones when observing the moving shadow cast by a tree beyond the threshold of his cave.

The next development was to stick a pole in the ground – to replicate a tree – and make marks in the earth at regular intervals so you had the beginning of a system of 'mechanical time', although at this primitive stage no mechanics were involved; instead, it was all down to the passage of the sun and shadows cast by poles.

The twelve-hour protocol was, Herodotus says, handed down to us by the Babylonians. Ever since, the urge to dissect time has been a part of civilised life . . . and its discontents. Without a sense of passing time, it would be impossible to be regretful about the past and fearful of the future. The sundial, it must therefore be admitted, was an invention which begat unmeasurably huge and oppressive volumes of anxiety.

So, what could be more natural to a poetic mind, a mind moved by the inevitable tragedy of passing time ('man fleeth as a shadow'), than to attach moralising mottoes to sundials, brief sentences or couplets to arouse thought while wondering what time it is.

'Time wastes our bodies and our wits
But we waste time and so we are quits'

From an old sundial

Charles Darwin had strong views about wasting time, feeling that to do so devalued life. Although I think it deserves to be said that Darwin's concept of 'waste' was formed in the crucible of Victorian capitalism when life was thought so cheap that children were sent down mines and up chimneys.

And it also needs to be said that this man to whom nature seems to have yielded all its secrets was, perversely, a physical wreck, a sufferer from an appalling catalogue of ailments, including dyspnea (shortage of breath), nocturnal intestinal gas, nervous exhaustion, colic, cramps, bloating, vertigo, depression and mouth ulcers. Modern medicine suggests all of these are symptoms of lactose intolerance, but I have a feeling they are also symptoms of an overly busy individual who felt staring out of the window was a waste of time rather than a very good way to *spend* time.

If I see two damsel flies mating above the pond, I am inclined to think what a delightful thing. Darwin was more inclined to want to analyse the life cycle of the Zygoptera. I am not one to disavow scientific or intellectual scrutiny, even if I encourage scepticism about the absolute nature of truths, wherever they are found, but in this case there is something to be said for my argument. There is an art to lassitude, a real skill in doing nothing. *'Dolce far niente'* is the happy Italian expression. How sweet it is to do bugger all. During The Great Isolation, I made friends with a pigeon. Staring at the damselflies or out of the window, you can think how lazily time creeps about. That's not wasting time but appreciating its real value.

'A poor life this if, full of care,
We have no time to stand and stare.'

W.H. Davies, 'Leisure' (1911)

Spending time is better than saving time. Whoever thought it a good idea to 'save time in the kitchen' when the

Reading in the Toilet
Or the pleasures of privacy

During The Great Isolation, reading was rediscovered.

To a scientist, reading is a complex cognitive process which involves both the construing of written words and also a journey to conceptual layers beneath the lexical surface. But to the aesthete, reading is a sacrament, an act of piety, a pleasure.

The tomb of Eleanor of Aquitaine in Fontevraud Abbey, near Chinon, has her, horizontal, reading a book. Clearly, it was what the queen consort of both France and England, one of the richest women on Earth, wanted to do in Heaven.

But the book has had a precarious history in the past century. George Orwell feared books might be banned in his fearful vision of a totalitarian future. Aldous Huxley, whose own vision of the future was a little more optimistic than Orwell's, suggested that the real danger was people no longer wanting to read in his *Brave New World*, since stupefying pleasure may come from other sources. Both were wrong.

Ten years ago, there was excitable talk about e-readers, but they have taken off only insofar as flying cars have taken off. The technology works, but the public is not yet wholly convinced. Of course, you still *read* with an e-reader, but it is a diminished experience. People prefer books.

'It is a thrilling experience to read [*Don Quixote*] today, when the very act of reading has been condemned to the dust heap of history by the gloomy prophets of the electronic millennium, with a goodly assist from the writers of the unreadable, the no-language of the ad man and the acronymic beeps of the bureaucrat, and the unquestioning clichés of the sensational best-seller.'

Carlos Fuentes writing on Cervantes in 1977

Reading is a sacrament that is a keen pleasure and completely free. To the Roman poet Martial, it could be as powerfully erotic as it was to Roland Barthes, who sometimes confused a good read with a dizzying orgasm.

Kirill Ryzhov/123rf.com

Henry Miller made 'Reading in the Toilet' a polemical chapter in his quasi-autobiographical *The Books in My Life* (1951).

Recommending his own *Epigrams*, the Roman influencer Martial was not afraid to suggest the latent erotic power lurking (not all invisible) in his lines: 'O how many times will you hammer your tunic with the swelling of your member . . . And you too, my girl, will read the games and indecency in this book of mine, wet between the legs.' Quite so. And he added mysteriously, 'Even if you are from Padua.' I have tried to research this Padua reference, but my efforts were inconclusive.

Writing on Sir Thomas Browne, the greatest prose stylist of his own day (who died in Norwich in 1682), Virginia Woolf said, 'The desire to read, like all other desires which distract our unhappy souls, is capable of analysis.' But what should that analysis be? Dante and Shakespeare require no defence, but how to judge less-celebrated work? How to distinguish quality from mediocrity?

Philip Larkin's advice is helpful: could I read it? If I could read it, did I enjoy it? And if I enjoyed it, how deep was that enjoyment and was it lasting?

Larkin's helpful guide is not, however, entirely foolproof. Few people would say Aleksandr Solzhenitsyn's *Gulag Archipelago* is anything other than a masterpiece . . . and even fewer would say it was enjoyable.

Less poetic was Mortimer Adler's *How to Read a Book*, published in 1940: a title in that American culture of Dale Carnegie's *How to Win Friends and Influence People*. Adler suggested three stages in the process of reading well. One: what have we got here? A blood-and-guts horror story or a dissertation about the evolution of the flute in Seicento Mantua? Two: ask yourself what is the plot, what is the argument? Three: what merit is there in the author's treatment?

'Some books are to be tasted, others to be swallowed, and some few to be chewed and digested: that is, some books are to be read only in parts; others to be read, but not curiously; and some few are to be read wholly, and with diligence and attention. Some books may also be read by Deputy, and Extracts of them made by others. But that would be only in the less important arguments, and the meaner sort of books: else distilled books are like common distilled waters, flashy things.'

Francis Bacon

The actual act of reading is for most people a keen pleasure, even if it often falls a little short of Martial's Roman smut or Roland Barthes's orgasmic reverie (as might, alas, be the case here).

Despite a lot of specialist trumpeting, sales of e-books have been disappointing, at least to those who anticipated the death of print as electrons succeeded pigments held in liquid suspension imprinted on processed cellulose fibres. Why? Because the physical presence of the analogue book is in itself valuable: as well as being instructive or entertaining, a book can (or must) also be beautiful. As the novelist Anthony Powell averred, 'books do furnish a room'. You can't say that of a digital Kindle.

Indeed, so much so that the arrangement of books is a revelatory presentational device, a performative act to be actively deployed and to be passively enjoyed. During the brief efflorescence of Zoom during The Great Isolation, many people paid very, very careful attention to the books in the background.

Personally, I shuffle the visible examples of the large art books in our drawing room in anticipation of guests' arrival. Sometimes the intention is to impress, sometimes to confuse. I mean to say, as a visitor, what inference would you make about a host who had a Morris Minor workshop manual next to Erwin Panofsky's *Early Netherlandish Painting* and a lush album of Pirelli-calendar nudes?

In the same way as Bernard Berenson felt great art and architecture communicated to him often at a sub-conscious level, books do not have to be read. At least, not immediately. I have always had a suspicion that possession of a book is in itself a way to enjoy its value, even before it is actually read. Umberto Eco rather agreed: he built his library from books that he *might* one day find useful, a sort of futures market in ideas. And, of course, good books have a lasting value way beyond the irrelevance of their original cost.

'Reading in the Toilet' is a chapter in Henry Miller's *The Books in My Life*, a curious publication of 1951. Here, two sacraments – the privacy of evacuation and the enjoyment of a book – are brought together. Here, the bolt on the loo door achieves a special significance, as will be made clear a little later.

Henry Miller (1891–1980)

Miller invented a new style of autobiographical fiction, a pre-cursor of the New Journalism. 'Uncensored, formless, fuck everything' was the way he put it. His novel *Tropic of Cancer* was published in Paris in 1934 but banned in the United States until 1961 on account of an obscenity that still shocks today.

Miller was a bold contrarian and knew very well that reading in the toilet was not a subject that had been treated often by writers or thinkers. While he thought taking a seat in the public library was like 'taking a seat in heaven', bolting the loo door and getting down to a good picture magazine, a detective story or a thriller was 'a minor form of bliss'.

We read, he explained, for five reasons. To get away from ourselves (always difficult in a toilet). To protect ourselves from real or imaginary dangers (and here the water closet surely comes into its own). To impress others (under normal circumstances unlikely in a loo). For information; and for enjoyment.

But he was only a cautious advocate of toilet reading. He advised restraint and care, awarding points for self-editing reading matter. He said you must always ask yourself if you really need to read while exercising bowels because 'I am certain that no author, not even a dead one, is flattered by associating his work with the drainage system'.

Instead, Miller advocates that the period spent in what he called the John was most wisely spent calculating what exactly to do with one's free time.

'The first ships to leave the earth, and possibly never return – what I would not give to know the titles of the books it will contain! Methinks the books have not been written which will offer mental, moral and spiritual sustenance to these darling pioneers. The great possibility, as I see it, is that these men may not care to read at all, not even in the toilet: they may be content to tune in on the angels, to listen to the voices of the dear departed, to cock their ears to catch the ceaseless celestial song.'

Henry Miller, *The Books in My Life* (1951)

Crapola

The ordinary and the exquisite

Finding value in ordinary things is a keen pleasure.

Take escalators, for example, so easy for subway-using urbanites to take for granted. The late Peter Campbell, designer of the *London Review of Books*, wrote a mesmerising essay about escalators which was published on 7 March 2002.

It is too elaborate an account to summarise here and, besides, a summary would not do justice to its almost mystically hallucinogenic quality. You, the reader, need to become enchanted by Campbell's insights into the mechanisms of the escalator and how they have influenced both human behaviour and the shape and conduct of cities. His point, I think, was that if you can understand how something works, you understand everything about it. You need to interrogate things to understand their inherent poetry.

But for instance, on the London Tube, escalators run at a maximum speed of 145 feet per minute. If they go any faster, people are reluctant to use them and any theoretical improvement by higher speed is made nugatory by fear. There's a metaphor waiting to emerge there.

Lift Versus Stairs

All mechanisms for vertical transport have their pains and their pleasures, a natural consequence of hubristically denying gravity. But surely the passenger lift is the scariest device in our catalogue of dubious conveniences. Claustrophobia? Tick! Social proximity to the contagious and malodorous? Tick! Possibility of a nauseating and fatal plunge? You got it! And then there is the horror-movie uncertainty of what waits beyond the doors as they slide apart with agonising slowness. Axe murderers? Poison gas? Infernos? And to this can be added the vanity problems associated with reflections observed in mirrors under harsh lighting. The music? Designed to induce calm, but in fact productive of murderous anxiety. Let's not forget the disturbing twangs and judders and the prospect of being stuck between floors and desperately needing a pee while the firemen are on strike. On the whole, stairs seem a better option. Improve your cardio and gain a psychological advantage over others by taking two steps at a time. And arrive with a glow arising from a winning combination of raised temperature and smugness.

Escalators are models of efficiency. Manufacturers supplying London's Tube are contractually obliged to achieve 98 per cent availability, this for a mechanism whose step chains, guide channels and comb plates are in Sisyphus-like motion, running twenty hours a day for 364 days a year. Because foreign objects can be invasively destructive, TfL requires workers to double-bag small metal items such as nuts and bolts. But, of course, escalators do, occasionally, go out of order. This inspired Campbell to ruminate: 'Can broken ones be read as a symptom of malaise?' I think absolutely yes they can.

Everything can be read!

> ### McAndrew's Dream
>
> In 1894, Rudyard Kipling published a poem about a Scottish marine engineer called McAndrew who saw in his ship's engine room – with its mighty pistons and thrust shafts – a metaphor of the Universe: 'From coupler-flange to spindle-guide, I see Thy Hand, O God'. And there was 'Predestination in the stride o' yon connectin'-rod'. Of course there was.

'Prime minister, please tell me your understanding of how a rivet works' is a question I have long wanted to ask. But, alas, never have.

I think the Rivet Test is a good one. Anyone can be tested. And anyone who cannot explain that a rivet is a mechanical fastening with a head and a tail is not, I believe, to be trusted. Moreover, the thing about rivets is that they require teamwork: there are certain installation protocols that cannot be ignored. The rivet also has its own vocabulary: it's worth knowing what a buckle and a mandrel are.

Like any great technique – fresco, for example – riveting has its disciplines, its masters and pupils, its agreed language. I do not understand how anyone could tolerate living in a world whose processes they made little effort to understand. By all means criticise air travel, but your criticism would have more heft if you were able to explain the principles of bypass gas flow, second-stage compressors and hybrid-laminar flow controls.

The Rivet Test is simply a device to encourage a thoughtful scrutiny of ordinary stuff.

The great authority on Italian wine Victor Hazan was eloquent about the virtues of a boiled potato. Provided of course that it was a perfectly boiled potato. With that condition met, to Hazan (who lived in very great comfort in the Cannaregio *sestiere* of Venice) the ordinary can become sublime.

The cartoonist Art Spiegelman would have agreed. Like John Updike, he wanted to give the everyday its beautiful due. Kidney stew, Spieglemann argued, can be divine.

'My artistic deficiencies remove me from the sphere of Rembrandt and Michael Angelo. My ever-present realisation of the material virtues of kidney stew and gorgonzola cheese has permanently destroyed whatever of the ethereal that may have been born within me . . . A touch of art may nourish the soul, but a good laugh always aids the digestion.'

Art Spiegelman, reported in *The New Yorker* (2020)

The painter Philip Guston, at a moment when his career seemed to have stalled, coined the very helpful term 'crapola' to describe the fascinating grunge of the American landscape: the motels, truck stops, gas stations and strip malls. Banality is here tipped towards the epic by the memory of a thousand movies, the melancholy paintings of Edward Hopper, and the deadpan photographs of Stephen Shore and Ed Ruscha. It used to be called cacotopia, but I think crapola is more resonant, as it sounds more like the name of a branded product. More valuable a term too, since it contains simultaneous senses of disgust and wonder. A terrific bit of branding, Phil.

There is beauty in crap (for eyes trained to see).

So much of the American landscape shows the intervention of man. Even in the most apparently virgin territory. You can see this flying from London to Los Angeles. If it is a clear day, over Bismarck, South Dakota, you can marvel at the majestic rectangular patchwork of fields created by a presidential *fiat* of long ago. This was a sight that was never seen before the twenties when air travel became a popular reality and people could gaze in wonder.

Soon, passengers would fly over the Grand Canyon. No one is gainsaying the impression the Grand Canyon makes. But I don't think it blasphemous to say that the field patterns of South Dakota are beautiful, while the awful chasm in Arizona is sublime. The hand of man creates a gentle beauty? The force of nature boggles us stupendously?

The word 'landscape' comes from the Dutch '*landschap*', which actually means a functional unit of land rather than the beautiful view it has come to suggest. Of course, it is not difficult to admire a conventional landscape, with its rolling greenery and hazy distances, but then you ask yourself what exactly are the conventions?

Most of what we regard as 'natural' was an invention of the eighteenth century when the Earls of Creation – Burlington, Pembroke, Leicester, Oxford and Bathurst – set about relocating truculent peasants, drowning villages and blocking rivers to recreate in England a fanciful vision of an Arcadia – an Edenic bliss – glimpsed while travelling in the Roman *campagna* or seen in the pictures of Claude Lorraine or Gaspar Dughet.

These repatriated Grand Tourists brought an end to the formal garden. Instead, with their fascination for the accidents of Italy, they turned nature itself into a spectator experience at least as artificial as the M25 or Brunel's Clifton Suspension Bridge.

The great apologist for seeing value in the man-made American landscape was the geographer John Brinckerhoff Jackson (1909–1996). His career began as an intelligence officer with the 9th Infantry Division of the US Army, analysing the topography of a Europe just sensing liberation after D-Day. But soon Jackson's investigations went beyond military duty. He collected picture postcards, printed ephemera and tourist guides. He interviewed Wehrmacht captives and collated all this information with aerial photographs to create extraordinarily richly textured pictures of the landscape. He published an essay called 'Landscape as seen by the Military'. In 1951, he founded a journal called *Landscape*, and landscape he defined as 'a complex and moving work of art, the transcript of a significant collective experience'.

A privileged individual, Jackson was almost dogmatically in favour of intrusions into nature made first for the benefit of the common man and second, he passionately argued, for the benefit of all of us. This he felt dignifying and empowering. He was not at all interested in 'Nature Mysticism' (although he liked trees). He enjoyed crowded ball parks and preferred commercial wood lots to primeval forest. Route 66 was at least as interesting as the Colorado River.

This was the beginning of what's become known as cultural geography, a discipline Jackson made his own. He wanted us to enjoy 'the full imprint' of man on nature. Commuting and zoning fascinated him. Every time he arrived in a new town, he would consult the telephone directory and calculate the proportion of, say, beauticians to doctors. This to get that textured picture of his surroundings.

The wild territory he wanted to explore was the ordinary American town whose affinity for the horizontal he shared.

For Jackson, the human impact was always beautiful: power lines enhanced the view, and he was positively fascinated by the loading bays trucks used at their depots, something he wrote about at impressive length. And he loved cars. Which came first, he wanted to know: the house or the road leading to the house? Environmentalists were reactionaries.

It impressed Jackson that so much did Americans revere the culture of roads that even in the chaos of the 1992 Los Angeles riots people obeyed red traffic lights. 'Roads belong in a landscape,' he wrote. He admired the botanist Edgar Anderson, who took his students on field trips to study the weeds that grew on spoil tips.

A rich man and a Harvard professor, late in life Jackson joined an African church, got a set of jailhouse tatts and became a qualified car mechanic. This he regarded as 'learning to be civilised'. His last employment was being the 'clean-up guy' at a garage in Albuquerque. This he found more valuable than golf.

'[We must in considering the landcape] differentiate among those wounds inflicted by greed and destructive fury, those which serve to keep us alive, and those which are inspired by a love of order and beauty, in obedience to some divine law.'

John Brinckerhoff Jackson,
A Sense of Place, A Sense of Time (1994)

I take the spirit of J.B. Jackson with me wherever I go. He is the most reliable guide to finding value everywhere . . . if you are prepared to look.

In his 1999 classic of collector's monomania *Boring Postcards*, Martin Parr, a photographer who romanticises distress, displays a genius for man-made ugliness. He reproduces the interchange of I-75, I-85 and I-20 in Atlanta. A bridge over the Pennsylvania Turnpike is in frank contradiction with the nostrums of functionalist theory which claim that engineering is inevitably beautiful. Well, as Parr shows, sometimes it is not.

One postcard is even called 'Travelling on Beautiful Interstate 35'. No life, not even traffic, is on show. The blue sky has puffy clouds, and the photographer has planted his tripod on the centre line in the middle of the highway to achieve an effect of perfectly symmetrical and stultifying banality. A clunking concrete bridge lies heavily across the road. The grass is green but looks artificial. Strange, really, how it is possible to write even as much as this about so very little.

Clouds: An Aside

Clouds are a modern invention, more or less contemporary with the steam engine and the gaslight. Of course, clouds existed in history, but the great artists of, say, the Renaissance painted them without much discrimination. They were fluffy, white-grey generics. It was as if Giovanni Bellini had never really looked at the sky. But the nineteenth century, with its urgent taste for classifying things, decided to understand high-altitude water vapour in a scientific style. This was the work of Luke Howard, a pharmacist from Tottenham. Howard was the very first person to stare upwards and distinguish one cloud from another. Or, at least, the first person to do so and to coin an unforgettable vocabulary to describe what he saw. His are the terms 'cirrus', 'cumulus', 'nimbus' and so on, still with us today. It was a perception of unique synoptic genius, more magnificent even than Admiral Beaufort's identification of the different states of the sea (also unimproved since its invention).

And with this classification came a cascade of meanings and metaphors. Howard's sketches of clouds were an explicit influence on John Constable, Britain's greatest landscape painter. In a Constable picture, for the first time in history, clouds are depicted with observational accuracy. Additionally, they are agents of mood. Since a cloud no bigger than a man's hand predicted the Biblical flood, clouds have had a metaphorical value: in Constable they can be menacing or delightful. 'Storm clouds gathering' is a lazy cliché but conveys a sense with absolute clarity. And, since their discovery, clouds have been a valuable stimulus to metaphor. People talk about 'blue-sky thinking' to suggest unimpeded thought, but clear blue skies do very little to stimulate anybody who actually lives underneath them . . . as any visitor to cloudless Los Angeles knows. A more vapid culture cannot be imagined. The city's greatest painter, Ed Ruscha, had to take his inspiration from commercial typography and gas stations. Blue skies mean tedium.

The narrator in Saul Bellow's *Henderson the Rain King* talks of flying above the clouds and getting a privileged view available once only to the gods. Joni Mitchell turned this insight into the song 'Both Sides Now'. Flight allows us to see clouds from above *and* below, perspectives unavailable to artists of the Renaissance, giving you and me a view superior to Giovanni Bellini's. Clouds mean weather and weather is *interesting*. Clouds create not just weather but illusions too. The contrails left by high-altitude aircraft are artificial weather as well as poignant graphics of international travel. Astonishing, really, to think that there are people up there in that silver speck leaving its snail-trail en route to somewhere far away from somewhere else even farther away.

> Who has ever looked at the sky and seen not cumulonimbus but an illusion of, shall we say, a bat-eared fox or a porcini mushroom? And then, like all illusions, the clouds rearrange themselves to become something else. The variety is endless. So too is the stimulation. A weather system with clouds in it keeps you alert: at this moment gratified, at another relieved, at yet another fretful or anticipatory. No one wants eight-eighths cloud cover, but nor does anyone want the featureless, stupefying cerulean vault above LA.
>
> Forget about blue-sky thinking. Clouds have silver linings. It's cloud thinking that needs to be encouraged.

The miracle of superhighways such as Interstate 35, according to P.J. O'Rourke, was that there were no views. At least, no views of conventional beauty. As Alice B. Toklas says, in Gertrude Stein's account, 'I like a view but I like to sit with my back turned to it'.

O'Rourke says natural beauty is boring: 'Scenery? Pah! You look at a beautiful vista and, all right, it's beautiful. Now what? After thirty seconds you begin to fidget. You wish you had a book, a Sony Walkman, even a Taco Bell double dogfood enchilada.' Besides, the other problem with nature's bounty as seen from a car travelling the Interstate even at a sedate fifty-five miles per hour is that 'swivel your head to capture the beauty and you'll hit a bridge abutment'.

Bentonville, Arkansas, is the home of Walmart. Here the injection of great wealth did little to reduce the banality of the scene. Yet such stupefying visual tedium has an almost mesmerising quality. O'Rourke celebrated the American's fundamental freedom to make everything look like shit, as he so nicely put it.

A sequence of cross-country road-trips made in the seventies allowed Peter Shire to record the epic banality of America's fly-over states.

What are we going to do about it, O'Rourke wanted to know: 'Are we going to bulldoze every Kmart and create a federal agency to design something in its place?'

Well, that's very nearly what Donald Trump proposed in 2020 when he signed an executive order mandating that in future all federal buildings should be in a classical style, so that an abacus and metope on a jail on Bumsville would give it dignity.

In contrast, O'Rourke saw value in 'Dairy Queens, water slides, flea markets, Cinema 1-2-3-4-5-6s . . . they are our family. They may be ugly and embarrassing, but we wouldn't be here without them. Americans just love this stuff.' So: Make America Crap Again.

Thus, the Zen of crap. But would Far Horizons Trailer Village in Tucson or the Celanese plant between Kingsville and Bishop, Texas, be relieved of their ugly horror if nature overwhelmed them, if their concrete paths and pipe manifolds and distillation towers fell into desuetude and creepers covered the rusting metal and faded vinyl and other crap?

These natural softenings or improvements were the classic effects of ruin that Rose Macaulay described as 'enjungled' in her fetishised account of 1953, *Pleasure of Ruins*. She writes pleasurably about exploring a ruin and finding a bestiary of dragons, satyrs, screech-owls, serpents, speckled toads and foxes.

Today in a modern ruin, such as a landfill, we might find not Macaulay's trees thrusting through the empty window sockets, the rosebay and fennel blossoming within the broken walls, the brambles tangling outside. We will more likely find a stained microwave, some old tyres, plastic bottles and crisp packets. But *autres temps, autres moeurs.*

You might not experience Stendhal's Syndrome in front of a Texaco filling station, a KFC or a KwikFit, but architecture is a spiritual experience: the best raises the spirits; the worst lowers them. People are happy to stare at screens but unwilling to stare at their surroundings. But the continuous interrogation of the world about us is enthralling. I sometimes think it should be made compulsory.

Reading Buildings
Let the bricks speak

Since we are surrounded by them, it's easy to become blind to buildings. And, besides, most people never look above eye level, which means, since the majority of most buildings are above that height, a great many valuable architectural treats go unobserved. In fact, most buildings go unobserved. The way we walk blindly around cities is the approximate equivalent of swallowing food without chewing it.

But why wander the city in an unmediated fog of careless ignorance? There are alternatives, because you can do sightseeing close to home. And you can do it every day.

Looking at a building is not a passive act. Learning architectural vocabulary is a marvellous aid to understanding. Every time I look at a building, I test myself by asking if I could write a prose paragraph about its appearance sufficiently accurate that an illustrator could immediately visualise it. Nikolaus Pevsner and Ian Nairn were consummate masters at doing this: Pevsner with an austere and precise vocabulary; Nairn with a Guinness-flavoured genius at metaphor and allusion.

If you don't know what an abacus is or how a cantilever works or why Flemish bond brickwork is different to English bond, then you are the poorer for it. You should be ashamed if you do not know the difference between a sash, a casement and a transom window.

Understanding a building requires engagement – first of the senses, then of the intellect. You need to learn how to read it, both actually and metaphorically.

Try drawing a building. To draw a building is to understand it. Why? Because drawing is a function of intelligence. Perhaps a small one, but a function nonetheless. If you truly understand something as apparently simple as a terracotta flowerpot, then you should be able to draw it accurately. But most people cannot. This is probably because they have not been looking properly, but possibly because they are not very intelligent.

Anyway, if you can master a flowerpot, there is really no reason why you cannot next master Baldassare Longhena's Chiesa di Salute (that great monument on Venice's Grand Canal commissioned to celebrate the city's deliverance from a plague of its own). But choose any building. If anything was going to test your powers of analysis, this would be it.

First, some scrutiny and careful contemplation are required – perhaps the Longhena church requires and deserves more of both than the local KFC, although each has a language of its own. When you look at any building, ask the simple questions: what were the designer's intentions? How well did he realise them? Precisely what effect does it have on me?

Then the detailed cross-examination can begin. Most buildings are designed on some sort of geometrical grid. What is it? And what are the rules the designer is working with (or choosing to ignore)? In the medieval period, the mason's rule dictated proportions. In Baroque Venice, it was a fantastical reinterpretation of the classical orders of architecture. More recently, steel stanchions and concrete floorplates dictate the geometry upon which the architect then adds an overlay to satisfy the vanity and ambition of the developer.

'In Venice the world is stone. There, in stone, to which each changing light is gloss, the human process shines clear and quasi-permanent. There, the lives of generations have made exteriors, acceptable between sky and water, marbles inhabited by emotion, feelings turned to marble.'

Adrian Stokes, *The Stones of Rimini* (1934)

Conventionally, the elevation of a buildings is conceived by its designer in terms of 'bays', which are formal units of measure. But remember even the meanest KFC is not mere structure but has an element of poetry about it. Not fine poetry, perhaps, but something struggling to express itself.

When looking at a 'facade', remember that this word really means 'face'. And it's true: buildings reveal their authentic character and quality only after detailed study, but their face is also greeting you. What exactly is it saying?

And the windows may, if it does not seem too glib, be compared to eyes on a human face. What part do they play in determining the building's character? And what about the details? Are they arbitrary or well considered? Executed with care or carelessly? Then ask similar questions about the materials.

Always remember: very little is accidental. No matter how dismaying or exalting a building might be, almost everything you are looking at was done on purpose. And it's every person's civilised duty to understand that purpose.

And style? Style should perhaps not come last. Then, again, perhaps it should. Longhena's glorious Baroque works well in the magical light of Venice, but would it be so effective in the grey miasma of Aberdeen? Check those shadows! And while drawing any building, always ask yourself 'how might it be improved?'

How to Become an Architecture Critic

1. Look at a lot of buildings.

2. Spend time in these buildings. (Most architectural awards are nonsense because they are based on superficial appraisal of appearance alone.)

3. Ask yourself the following:

Q: Does this building move me?

Q: If yes, in exactly what direction?

Q: And am I pleased to be taken there?

Q: How do the spaces, materials and details affect my mood?

Q: How might it be better?

That's all.

And when you have completed a drawing of a single building, just consider how rewarding it would be to draw an entire city.

Think how much power and understanding that would realise. How very valuable that would be. When he was reluctantly leaving Palermo in June 1953, Bernard Berenson wrote from the heights of Monte Pellegrino, **'If only one could possess it all and keep it, one would be a god.'** Thing is, you can. I mean you can possess it, and you can, following the argument, become a god. Even on a wet Tuesday in Lewisham.

I'd suggest carrying a sketchbook everywhere – it raises IQ – but especially when walking and night-walking cities. T.S. Eliot's mournful Prufrock – measuring out his life in coffee spoons once again – saw only lonely men in shirt sleeves on his doleful urban rounds, but a man with a sketchbook sees more and is never really alone.

And before this passage ends, are you sure you know the proportions of a London stock brick or a traditional sash window? Test yourself by drawing a Georgian facade from memory. It's a very valuable (and humbling) exercise.

Picturing It
Great art reveals itself slowly

It really can't be stated more simply: engaging with great art is an exceptionally valuable thing to do. If you ask me, engaging with great art is one of the essential purposes and most satisfyingly enjoyable aspects of civilised life.

Of course, there are different sorts of and degrees in 'greatness', but we'll come to that later. Still, at its best, an engagement with art is very similar to, possibly even better than, a religious experience and one that's available to those inclined to the secular rather than to piety.

But the major art galleries are not places where contemplative engagement is much encouraged or even actually possible. Mostly descended from Victorian institutions whose purpose was to demonstrate the depth of the patron's generosity, the scope of his taste or, alternatively, the municipality's high intentions for civic life, collections tend to be confusingly eclectic and arranged in a way that pays more attention to old-fashioned curatorial turf wars than to aesthetic gratification.

And the possibilities for engagement are further reduced when the successful galleries of the world tend to be given over to Disneyfied visitor experiences, orientation rooms, coffee concessions, gift shops, queuing for headline exhibitions guiltily sponsored by accountancy firms (as a sort of expiation) or to act as holding pens for listless tour parties who are really only interested in the American Hot pizza that will come later as a reward for diligent, if painful, exposure to culture. The great art historian John Richardson, biographer of Picasso, said the most depressing noise in the world was the sound of cash registers as you entered New York's Metropolitan Museum.

Within any great museum, crocodiles of bum bags are briefly stalled before the acknowledged masterpieces; usually, audio guides are clamped to zombie heads whose eyes look but do not actually see. You see a sort of vacant engagement on the faces, a mute registration of smooth information which carries little revelatory force. And then the crocodile, unenthusiastic, but nonetheless determined, shuffles off to the next masterpiece. And any notion that art has a sacred quality is tested to near destruction.

These melancholy circumstances can be found anywhere on earth where tourism is practised: the Prado in Madrid, New York's Metropolitan Museum, the Uffizi in Florence, London's National Gallery or, most notably, the Louvre in Paris. This last is the world's most-visited art gallery. The stats would make an astrophysicist pause: the bum bags are in the many millions and rising. But the Louvre is one of the worst places on earth to engage with art. Engaging with art in the Louvre is as futile as reading a sonnet in a football crowd.

One way out of this is to ignore the galleries and make a dedicated pilgrimage to see a single great work of art in – or very near – the place it was intended to be. Like driving a Jeep through Monument Valley, engaging with art in its place of origin has a special value. Surely, this is the best justification for any sort of travel.

And if the word 'pilgrimage' has religious associations, that's entirely deliberate, since versions of religious application and religious susceptibility are necessary for full value to be realised here.

This is what Peter Schjeldahl of *The New Yorker*, the most perceptive art critic since Robert Hughes, did when he knew he was dying. He chose to make a pilgrimage to Madrid's Prado to see Velázquez's *Las Meninas* of 1656 for the last time and to dedicate himself to – eventually – understanding its many mysteries. He said he would give it as long as it takes . . . because while it is almost always immediately possible to sense you are in the presence of great art, the very greatest art reveals its secrets only slowly.

Las Meninas – which means 'ladies in waiting' – is one of the most enigmatic pictures in the entire history of art. It is contextually and visually ambiguous to a degree that has had art historians in a frightful flummox of interpretation, with no single explanation yet dominant. But all are agreed, it is a painting about painting.

For example. Whose eyes are we seeing from? Not the painter himself, because he is there on the left. But what is he painting? Presumably a double portrait of Philip IV and Mariana of Austria, whose hazy reflections can be seen in a mirror at the back. But does this mean the painting is showing us what the King of Spain himself sees? Perhaps. Who knows? We must decide.

But *Las Meninas* has often been described as the ultimate demonstration of what painting on canvas can achieve. A fine subject for contemplation by a great, yet tragically moribund, art critic. At this stage in his life, Schjeldahl had no need of money but a great need for this superlative picture.

Great paintings reveal themselves only slowly. But what's the hurry?

Since the greatest art yields itself only after time-consuming contemplation and Schjeldahl was mortally ill, he was in a predicament with little time to spare. After days of contemplation (in the maddening bustle of the Prado), he understood more and wrote about it beautifully ... but he had to confess that he did not understand everything. Great art plays a long game.

There are many other options besides Velázquez, but consider, perhaps, the stupendous *Adoration of the Mystic Lamb* by Jan van Eyck, still in the chapel of the cathedral of St Bavo in Ghent where it first astonished worshippers in 1434. The scale and ambition of this altarpiece, to say nothing of its technical accomplishment, are different to anything hitherto seen in Northern Europe. Or, to be honest, anywhere else.

Today, if you arrive in Ghent in a comfortable air-conditioned car, it's a short walk from the parking to the first sight of the *Mystic Lamb*, which is suddenly awesome and humbling and life-changing, even to the most worldly twenty-first-century individual. Imagine, then, what it must have been like to a fifteenth-century Flemish peasant who lived with his pigs in a wattle-and-daub hovel, existing on a diet of gruel with the occasional thieved rabbit for pot luck.

This unwashed peasant, who would have walked ten uncomfortable miles to visit St Bavo, his feet wrapped in rough felt, would never before have seen so many vivid colours, never experienced such polished surfaces. There was very little colour or polish in his life. Van Eyck's altarpiece would have been no less than a presentiment of Heaven itself.

Or perhaps visit Colmar, in Alsace in eastern France (just down the road from the famous Ribeauville vineyards), where in the Musée d'Unterlinden there is Matthias Grünewald's *Isenheim Altarpiece*. The museum is not far from the Monastery of Saint Anthony, where this painting, one of the most astonishing in the Western canon, originally stood.

Matthias Grünewald's *Isenheim Altarpiece* of 1516 is an illustration of skin disease which demonstrates how compelling – even beautiful – 'ugliness' can be.

The Hospital Brothers of Saint Anthony were followers of St Anthony (251–357), patron saint of Gubbio, who was the founder of Christian monasticism and lived a life of solitude in a cave (near modern Dayr al-Maymnū), where he confronted his many and restless demons.

Anthony used austerity to battle his spiritual foes. This principled stand was an inspiration to the many painters who fashioned ever more horrible torments for Anthony, a subject also treated by Hieronymus Bosch. As a result, St Anthony was often invoked by sufferers from skin disease, who gained access to the saint through solemnising flowerpots of *l'erba di San Antonio* by placing them in sunlight.

Certainly, the crucified Christ in Grünewald's painting is in a shocking condition. Some have identified his complaint as herpes, but his affliction is more likely the medieval physician's St Anthony's Fire. This is now recognised as ergotism, a fungal poisoning that creates in its victims spasms, convulsions, psychosis, oedemas, hallucinations, gastroenteritis and dry gangrene.

It was common, which is not to say popular, in the Middle Ages. Sufferers felt as if they were being burnt alive and, just to make it worse, fingers, toes and hands might drop off. The unsurprising result was that ergotism produced a sort of delirious madness. (With a small imaginative leap, it's almost possible to sense the smell of disease and decay: pox, polecats and mortuaries. Heaven, by contrast, smelt good.)

Grünewald's Christ presents all these symptoms frankly and shockingly. See it on a pilgrimage and enjoy the valuable sense of security that modern healthcare can sometimes bring.

A similar dedicated pilgrimage could be made to, say, Monterchi in Tuscany to enjoy Piero della Francesca's *Madonna del Parto* in the tiny village museum where it was recently installed after five hundred years in a nearly neglected roadside shrine. To many, this unique image of the pregnant Madonna is the single most beautiful picture ever painted. Or perhaps visit Toledo to see El Greco's bizarre *Burial of the Count of Orgaz*, which he finished in 1586. The psychedelic Mannerism of this unique work of art is not at all compromised by the gift shop selling plasticised kitchen aprons with the grey, dead count as the decorative motif to shocked Chinese tourists. The memory of the art survives the kitsch of the apron.

But this approach is not exclusive to Old Masters. It applies to Modern Vintage Masters as well. The pilgrimage exercise could be performed with Jackson Pollock; visit his house in East Hampton on Long Island and see where Jack the Dripper first flicked and poured his Duco enamel paint. Familiar now, but Pollock changed art, and in 1945 the effects he made his own had never been seen outside the accidental mess of an industrial paint shop. Pollock was, on his bad days, a lecherous drunk and a cruel bully, so I will not call him a Holy Man, but there is something sanctified in his house. And that's valuable.

But an alternative to the dedicated foreign pilgrimage as a route to gratifying engagement with art can be found closer to home. This involves choosing your art gallery and instead of attempting to engage with its entire baffling collection . . . edit it, because the vainglorious curators have refused to. Very few things do not benefit from being energetically edited, and art galleries are not excluded from that rule.

Simply select a single work of art and ignore the rest. Do not dally, ignore the visitor centre and any official attempts at 'orientation', and go straight to it. It can be a work you already know or one that you do not know at all.

If you are, for example, in Liverpool, perhaps choose a neglected masterpiece such as Giovanni Segantini's peculiar painting of 1891, *The Punishment of Luxury*. This was a childhood favourite of mine. 'Luxury' was originally 'Lust', and the iconography combines Alpine scenery, bohemian Milanese prostitutes and Buddhism. It is a picture you see once and never forget.

And it doesn't necessarily have to be a painting you like; on the contrary, the exercise might be even more valuable if you choose a work of art that does not immediately please you.

Finding value in something you do not actually like is a very rewarding experience.

Importantly, in the first instance, let the picture speak to you without interruption. It will, if you give it and yourself . . . time. And if the picture does not immediately speak to you, what you must do is interrogate it. (It's an important principle of art appreciation that if you don't like a picture, make yourself think what you would like about it if you did like it. This is, incidentally, a test of judgement that has great value outside the confines of an art gallery. It works on people too.)

But the important thing is to suspend judgement until the interrogation has taken place. Give it that time. Be patient. If you do not have days to spend, twenty minutes of contemplation before engaging any higher intellectual attributes would be my suggested minimum.

After twenty minutes, there are questions to be asked. Presuming, at this stage, that the painting you are looking at is a figurative one, rather than an abstract, the interrogation can begin.

The light. Where is it coming from? Is it artificial, natural or divine, and does it illuminate any characters or details in a significant way? If artificial, what is its source?

The weather. What is it doing? How is it creating a mood, or helping with the narrative? Perhaps there is no weather. But why? Now allow yourself to ask what effect the painting is having on you. If it is annoying you, try to understand exactly why. If it is pleasing you, do the same.

(Of course, if it is a Western painting made between, say, 1100 and 1870, it may have a complicated classical or Christian iconography. Eventually, understanding whether you are engaging with the Dormition of the Mother of God, the Ethiopian Eunuch, the Miracle of the Bees or St Julian Killing His Parents will add to the value of understanding, but right now that can wait: you can Google it later – it's important for now to keep seeing.)

It may be time to ask about the proportions of the canvas. Is there a reason the artist has preferred landscape to portrait? Was it convention or a creative decision? Composition is a subtle matter, but with rules widely understood by artists over the centuries, if no longer today. Google the 'Golden Section', '*Rabbatement* of the Rectangle' and the 'Law of Thirds' to see what I mean

Now the colours. What is the chromatic range? Remember that for most of the history of olden days' art, painters mixed their own colours, so what you see is not shop bought but an aesthetic decision. Velázquez's *Las Meninas* is predominantly brown, but that solemn fact does not stop it being one of the greatest pictures ever made.

The technique? Would you say it is loose or tight? Painterly or linear? How might it be different and to what effect? Always remember, nothing you are looking at is there by accident. Instead, it has been deliberately intended to create an effect. So, make sure you are still asking yourself what exactly that effect is.

And a similar approach works for non-figurative art, which is often designed for confrontation more than contemplation. The formal analysis of, say, a Donald Judd metal box may offer less immediate scope for analysis than a history painting of Deucalion and Pyrrha, but it is nonetheless demanding a response from you. Donald Judd may be minimal, but he is maximally in your face. What is your response . . . and was it worth having?

If there is any time left, ask yourself about the smells suggested by the picture. Velázquez? Surely dust, garlic, leather and sunshine. Pollock? Duco enamel, sweat, tobacco and stale beer.

With any engagement in art, you enter a world invented by the maker. And that is a valuable privilege, because the great mysteries of the world are the visible things, not the invisible ones. Mysteries always fascinate.

I would recommend learning a painting a day every day for a year so that – avoiding the crowds – 365 days later you have your own National Gallery in your head.

'My client is not in a hurry.'

> Antoni Gaudí explaining the delay in building
> La Sagrada Familia. (He took his client to be God.)

Late in life, as he was contemplating Velázquez, Peter Schjeldahl became fascinated by how insistent are the hints of mortality in Old Master paintings. There's an engaging paradox here, because the distinguishing mark of great art is always its *vitality*. And the thing about *kitsch* is that it is always . . . dead.

Say what you like about Jeff Koons (and I say his art is cynical, exploitative, pseudo-art garbage), but even his keenest investors cannot detect hints of mortality (or even of any spiritual content other than the love of money) in a brazen or inflated Koons. That said, Koons perfectly satisfies my definition of kitsch, which says it is the corpse that's left when vitality leaves art.

Hints of mortality give Old Masters more value, or 'heft', than even the most outstanding twentieth-century masterpiece. It's a matter of art outlasting life. You can put it another way, as an old sundial does: *Transit hora manent opera*. Time passes, but stuff remains.

Beauty Versus Ugliness
Ugliness may be superior because it lasts longer

At one level or another, doesn't everyone agree that the purpose of civilised existence is the identification, pursuit, consumption and, if at all possible, the production of beauty?

This is why diets and gyms, suntans, make-up and nail bars exist.

Why? Because beauty is a manifestation of the divine, whatever divinity might mean to you. Although it rather suggests that the taste for betterment is universal, the pursuit of perfection, or, at least, *improvement*, being on every agenda.

An aesthetic view of the world is not restricted to art galleries but can penetrate the wardrobe and kitchen as well. The garage too. Beauty can be found everywhere.

Seen with educated eyes, beauty can be a pick-up truck. Guns can be beautiful. Jean-Jacques Lequeu, the fantastical neoclassical architect, thought a woman's hips were the best inspiration for a beautiful moulding. Or beauty can be found in damage and decay as readily as it can be found in balanced perfection.

The important thing is to be always on the lookout for it.

Christopher Wren, architect of St Paul's, believed there

are two causes of beauty, which he described as 'natural and customary'. Natural beauty came from geometry; customary beauty came from a familiarity which makes us love things – or, I suppose, people – which are not in themselves lovely.

It's in architecture that aesthetics nudges into religion.

Marcel Proust said of John Ruskin, 'His one religion was that of beauty.' Ruskin's version of divinity, in Proust's words, was 'a reality infinitely more important than life itself, for which he would have given his own life'.

It might, for instance, mean the intuition of something mysterious. Surfaces and forms of plastic buckets and espresso cups may be important, but the suggestion that they represent a hidden and more fundamental truth gives those surfaces more value still.

The greatest intuition of all belonged to Michelangelo, whose vision penetrated the block of marble he was working on and he saw inside the stone a figure waiting to be set free by his sculptor's mallet. Because he could give life to marble, they called him 'Il Divino'.

'The Governor of Heaven . . . decided to redeem us . . . by sending to earth a spirit universally capable by single-handed effort in every art and profession, of exhibiting perfection: in the art of drawing, by delineating, outlining, shading and highlighting to give a painting a sense of three dimensions; as a sculptor, to work with right judgement; and in architecture, to make our dwellings comfortable and safe, sound, cheerful, well-proportioned, and rich in the variety of their ornament.'

Vasari on Michelangelo in
The Lives of the Artists (1550)

So, sitting in the arcaded loggia of a villa designed by Michelangelo (perhaps the one owned by the Agnelli family, owners of Fiat, in Pontedera, near Pisa), you might get a glimpse of Heaven and its possibilities.

'God had called him, and he had answered.'

Art historian Ingrid D. Rowland on Michelangelo in
The New York Review of Books (2020)

An appetite for beauty might even be *the* defining characteristic of civilisation. Why? Because most definitions of beauty already include indisputably civilised attributes such as harmony and peace.

But if there is a formula for beauty, someone would surely have found it by now. Although now we must say 'algorithm' and not 'formula', even if the new word is an uglier one. Surely, if it were possible to define it, someone would have managed to do so. It's been a long, long time since Plato.

The fact that it is so elusive does not make it less valuable. Quite the opposite.

One of the most useless and lazy tropes, mentioned here only to rubbish it, is that beauty is in the eye of beholder. Of course it is – basic neurology tells us so – but culture also tells us that there is a high level of agreement about what is and what is not beautiful.

Be that as it may, in 2021 an irreverent definition of beauty would be 'that which artists avoid'. Why? Because while for centuries artists made the pursuit and capture of beauty their more or less avowed business, today anyone identifying as an 'artist' would not want to have anything to do with it.

Artists no longer use the term 'beauty'. Does that mean it no longer exists? Or have we just given up the chase? Certainly, the standards by which beauty might be measured are so elusive it is tempting to suggest they might never be captured. Ugliness has its champions. Proust thought ugliness was aristocratic, since it suggested a lofty carelessness about pleasing an audience. Today, the architect Rem Koolhaas finds ugliness more interesting than beauty, without ever troubling to define either, although the Dutch architect's disturbing interest in ugliness is consistent: he once told the critic Edwin Heathcote that in restaurants he likes to order 'ugly food'.

The Ugly Test

Is it boring? Ugly stuff is usually rather fascinating. (It's beauty that tends to be dull.)

Is it aggressive or inviting?

Do I want more of it or less?

If I want less of it, exactly why?

Ask yourself precisely what is repulsive.

Is there a way to find some value in this unattractive experience?

Can it be improved and if so how?

Or is it irredeemable?

Beauty is, they say, easy to detect but impossible to define. But is that actually true? Can beauty be measured? Can we have too much of it?

One appealing definition is that something is beautiful if we want more of it. This was the basis for the best explanation of beauty. And so it is, at the same time, the best explanation of ugliness. The source is the literary critic Elaine Scarry, who says, **'Beauty brings copies of itself into being.'** We know something is beautiful if we want more of it, whether it is an attractive person or a desirable object. Professor Scarry's observation is acute, but Shakespeare did get there first. In Sonnet 1, he writes, 'From fairest creatures we desire increase,/That therefore beauty's rose may never die'.

Perhaps sensing beauty is the result of an editing process: look around you; exclude the dross. Get those wheelie bins out of my sight! Edit, edit, edit. And then decide if you want more of what's left after this process of visual subtraction. With great art, you return again and again.

But that still does not answer the question. Is physical beauty a mixture of proportions and purpose? Purpose gets us nowhere: John Ruskin said some of the most beautiful things in the world – lilies and peacocks were his example, but he had Victorian taste – were also entirely useless.

If functionality were a test of beauty, then the B–52 would qualify. But in his *Philosophical Enquiry into the Origins of Our Ideas of the Sublime and the Beautiful* of 1757, Edmund Burke has a wonderful passage about the functionality of the pig and how the farmyard animal fails the test for beauty: 'For on that principle, the wedge-like snout of a swine, with its tough cartilage at the end, the little sunk eyes, and the whole make of the head, so well adapted to its offices of digging and rooting would be extremely beautiful.' Similar arguments apply to monkeys, which are admirably calculated for running, leaping, grappling and climbing; and yet there are few animals which seem to have less beauty.

In nature and in science there is no clear relationship between functionalism and beauty . . . nor between efficiency and ugliness.

The essential argument in aesthetics is a very simple one, although professional philosophers are always reluctant to embrace simplicity in explanations, since to do so would be to render themselves redundant. As Burke himself believed, a clear idea is another name for a little idea.

Aesthetic Philosophers

I like what Henry Miller said about Hegel's *Phenomenology of Mind*: 'the acknowledged cornerstone of the whole nutcracker suite of intellectual hocus-pocus'. That was in *The Books in My Life* (1951). When George Orwell visited the sage Ying Chu in his cave, he was told, 'Most of your philosophising consists in trying to unravel the tangle that previous philosophers have made . . . Those who truly seek wisdom spend their days watching the river flow and listening to the birds singing. Their nights they devote to love.' At least, according to Gerald Brenan in *Thoughts in a Dry Season* (1978).

Anyway, the aesthetic argument is this. Is our response to beauty triggered by direct sensory inputs that a neurosurgeon could identify as blips on an oscilloscope? By which I mean, are there certain shapes, combinations of colours and texture which bypass conscious understanding and directly zap that part of the brain sensitive to beauty?

Or is our response to beauty triggered by associations, a conscious remembrance of delight experienced in another context. Take the 1971 Ferrari BB512 as an example. The 'BB', says its designer Leonardo Fioravanti, stands for Brigitte Bardot, whose remarkable poitrine became a source of international fascination when, in a landmark moment of cinema (if landmark is the right word), Roger Vadim filmed those twin peaks in a wet dress in his 1956 movie *Et Dieu Créa La Femme*. The Ferrari's curves ape Brigitte Bardot's.

Roger Vadim's 1956 film *Et Dieu Créa La Femme*, a celebration of sun, sex and sea, established the cult of St Tropez and launched the career of Brigitte Bardot.

Pictorial Press/Alamy Stock Photo

What you see in a Ferrari is a triumph of exceptionalism over ordinariness. Every detail has been conceived and executed with rapt attention. To visit the Museo Enzo Ferrari in Modena is to see this rapt attention applied to what's normally invisible: engines.

The setting is an old workshop where Ferrari engines are presented almost as objects for religious veneration, which, in several ways, they are. Old man Ferrari always said that the engines were what you paid for; the rest of the car he threw in for free.

You marvel at the almost indescribable effort put into castings, the strengthening webs and cooling vanes on crank cases, the vanity of a gorgeous red crackle-finish on the cam boxes. These things *speak* almost as if they were alive.

But this is a property not fully possessed by all cars and their components. A ten-year-old Jaguar looks moribundly dated because it was never an honest and lively proposition in the first place; it was always pretending to be something it was not (namely, a German car). But these Ferrari exhibits are absolute. Things unto themselves. They are copies of nothing and wholly inimitable.

A visit to the Museo Enzo Ferrari is the most extraordinary testament to human ingenuity, will and ambition. The exhibits exceed the ordinary in a fashion that is quite literally breathtaking. The absurdity and uselessness of it all, like Ruskin's lilies and peacocks, just make it more valuable still.

Q. Why?

A. Because, in the blind terror of a meaningless Universe, great designers and artisans have put emotional value into dumb materials. The Museo Enzo Ferrari shows what humans can achieve at their very best.

For many, it is one of the most beautiful collections in the world. And it's not even about cars, just about their means of propulsion.

How to Judge a Car Design

But car bodies are important too. More so with Ferrari than most: no other manufacturer has contributed so much to aggregates of beauty. Cars are mobile sculpture. Or perhaps mobile architecture. In less than a century, designers have established a set of techniques and traditions, as well as a vocabulary, which makes their craft at least the equal as a discipline to the routine practices of a Renaissance artist's atelier. It is all the more touching because soon it will be gone.

H-point: this, seen from the side elevation, is the point of the driver's hip; it is vital to establish this for the car's proportions and ergonomics.

Prestige gap: again, from the side elevation, the distance between the centre of the front wheel and the leading edge of the door. This is crucial in creating an elegant stance.

DTRG (Down the Road Graphics): studio jargon for the car's approaching 'face'.

DLO (Daylight Opening): the ratio of glass window to metal body is a designer's preoccupation.

Jewellery: the glittery bits; lights, chrome trim and so on.

Overhang: the distance between the wheel centres and the car's nose and tail. These affect the posture.

Character line: a longitudinal moulding which, handled correctly, can convey either athleticism or solidity.

Only one thing is certain in aesthetics: there is nothing simple about beauty.

The astonishing popularity of Quentin Matsys's 1512 portrait of Margaret of Austria in London's National Gallery demonstrates the curious law that ugliness is by no means necessarily repugnant. On the contrary, this grotesquely malformed woman, conventionally known as the 'Ugly Duchess', was the source for John Tenniel's scary illustrations of *Alice in Wonderland* which frightened literary children of long ago.

As admirers of Grünewald's *Isenheim Altarpiece* know, disease had a cruel fascination for painters of the northern Renaissance. The portrait was once assumed to be a fantastic grotesque, an imaginary composition inspired perhaps by Matsys's acquaintance with Leonardo da Vinci, who was fascinated by abnormality, as well as helicopters. But *The Ugly Duchess* is now thought to be a precise observation from nature. Paget's disease has been retrospectively diagnosed. This is a metabolic abnormality normally affecting the lower body, but here the sitter presents symptoms in her face. In this case the enlarged upper jaw has led to a hideously distended lip and a scrunched-up nose. Her forehead and chin are also distended and, one might assume, so too are the collarbone and arms.

Hideous? Of course, but it is among the most popular pictures with visitors to Trafalgar Square and is said to exceed Monet's pretty *Water Lilies* in postcard sales.

If it is curious that a portrait so ugly can be so popular, then there is the haunting paradox that if everything were beautiful, then nothing would be. Just as the existence of Satan has to be suspected in order to understand God, so the existence of ugliness is necessary for the appreciation of beauty.

Only one thing is certain in the history of taste: while an appetite for beauty is a constant, great art has no

permanent values, opinions change, preferences alter. There is no finality.

Writing about the 'religion of beauty' begs a lot of questions, and all the difficult ones I am going to duck. But the title of this passage is not so much a metaphor as a statement of fact. As is sometimes said, if you are perplexed and confused about the existence of God . . . then you have already found Him. Same with Beauty. If you are wondering how on earth it can be defined, you probably already know.

Going to Church with Le Corbusier
Making the bad difficult and the good easy

In the twentieth century, there were few more articulate spokesmen for beauty and its relationship to a type of religious experience than the architect Le Corbusier.

The next few paragraphs are not a history of his architecture. That's an enormous subject, and there are countless monographs that already do that. Some of them very well. Instead, Le Corbusier is here as a witness to the belief that the architect exists to bring practical, moral and aesthetic value to inert, dumb materials. And this is what he did with more bravura and better rhetoric than any architect before or since.

Le Corbusier Q&A

Q. Why did you abandon your family name of Jeanneret?

A I wanted to be like a solider with a *nom de guerre*.
But I chose a *nom d'artiste*.

Q. Tell me about drawing.

A. I prefer drawing to talking. Drawing is faster and leaves
less room for lies.

Q. What do you feel about the 'Simple Life'?

A. Space, light and order. These are the things men need
just as much as they need bread or a place to sleep.

Q. What is architecture?

A. The purpose of construction is to make things hold
together; of architecture, to move us.

Corb has his detractors, who are largely justified in their criticisms that he and his work can seem inhumane, authoritarian, bleak, but he remains the consummate example of what it is to be an architect (often described as the second oldest profession).

Some may advance Frank Lloyd Wright as an alternative in this role – he was, after all, probably the inspiration for the cheerfully demented Howard Roark in Ayn Rand's *The Fountainhead* of 1943. In the movie of the book, Gary Cooper became cinema's most infamous architect – but while Wright was as bombastic and lecherous as Corb, he was more limited as well. And much less influential.

To many, Le Corbusier remains a reviled technocrat, an unfeeling engineer of the soul who commanded that we live in machines.

'Une maison est une machine à habiter.'

Le Corbusier, *Vers une Architecture* (1923)

And if that sounds authoritarian, then it must be confessed that he openly admired Benito Mussolini and schmoozed Philippe Petain's Vichy government. True, fascists in Italy and Germany held the machine in as lofty a state of veneration as Corb himself. When he wrote '*L'avion accuse!*' (or 'the aeroplane points a finger'), he meant that lumpen, earthbound architects dulled by gravity's pull and with the limited resources of bricks and stone, could learn an awful lot from looking at the lightweight, efficient and beautiful structures of flying machines. Of course, fascists liked flying machines too.

He endorsed a 1935 book by Nobel Prize-winning surgeon Alex Carrel which advocated the gassing of a portion of the French nation to keep genetic quality high. With women, Corb was a hard dog to keep on the porch. He had affairs with Marilyn Monroe and, it was rumoured, Christine Keeler. He failed to nurture the reputation of his mistress–assistant Charlotte Perriand, who very likely designed the fabulous Jazz Age furniture routinely attributed to him.

Of his wife, Yvonne Gallis, a model, he said, 'She is pretty stupid, *mais quand-même*?' Or, 'so what?' After her cremation, he kept a part of her carbonised backbone in his back pocket, occasionally putting it on his work table for inspiration.

In a controversial and sensationalist book, the journalist Xavier de Jarcy described Le Corbusier's reputation as a 'great collective lie'. Certainly, his megalomania sometimes tipped towards fabulism: he made an outrageous claim that he was the source of the Citroën 2CV design. Certainly, I think we can agree that Le Corbusier is not susceptible to a single interpretation.

But Corb's political opportunism was really no more blameworthy than any architect making inevitable compromises in pursuit of a client. True, his reviled Plan Voisin for Paris, which called for the demolition of the historic Marais and its replacement by tower blocks and motorways, was insensitive, to put it no more extremely. But it was never built. It was a manifesto designed for suggestive purposes alone.

He had the restless vision of a great artist. And he was not afraid to remind people of this. His egotism was extreme. 'I am a greater artist than Picasso,' he told the *Manchester Guardian* in 1952.

But his love affair with machines was only a short one.

Even at the height of his infatuation with spigots, he wanted the occupants of his landmark Villa Savoie to be 'enfolded in a Virgilian dream'. His vision of this floating, white diagram of Jazz Age perfection at Poissy-sur-Seine was that the occupiers might think bucolic thoughts while showering in a bathroom with the plumbing made explicit.

Like all great artists, Corb quickly moved on – it's a definition of art that it evolve, while craft must always stay the same – from the brittle Jazz Age wonder of his *maisons blanches* to the astonishing expressive design language of his church at Ronchamp, designed in a way that no lexical language yet exists to describe it, certainly not the weary lingo of architectural criticism, then to the red-brick domesticity of his Jaoul houses at Neuilly, outside Paris.

If aircraft were an influence on his early aesthetic, humans were on his later art. His *Modulor* scheme of proportions was inspired by the mathematical system first described by Fibonacci: a sequence where a number is the sum of the two that preceded it. So far from being abstruse calculation, the Fibonacci numbers can be used to plot curves which also occur in natural forms.

Modulor

Le Corbusier's system of proportions – 'universally applicable to architects and mechanics' – was published in French in 1951. The English translation of three years later was by the painter Peter de Francia.

His relentless critics saw *Modulor* as a sinister attempt to reduce man to mathematics. But Albert Einstein, who Corb met at Princeton, said this system of proportions was valuable to architects and designers because it **'makes the bad difficult and the good easy'.**

And all the time Corb was influenced by religious architecture, particularly the three great Cistercian abbeys of Provence:

© Lucien Herve courtesy of Mme Judith Herve

Le Thoronet is one of the three great Cistercian monasteries of the Var. Its aesthetic is based in simplicity, light and silence.

Silvacane, Senanque and Le Thoronet, usually known as the 'Three Sisters'.

Medieval theologians thought beauty was evidence of God, and while no records exist to support the proposition, it's reasonable to believe that medieval masons believed that too. Anyway, I know no one in a position to deny it convincingly. Nice to believe that a shaft of light through a stained-glass window might – just possibly – be the Holy Ghost going about his work. And even if this is a delusion, what harm is there in believing it might be true?

Here in the silence and shadow, Le Corbusier found beauty and was inspired to write his sempiternal definition of architecture as 'the learned game, correct and magnificent, of forms assembled in light'.

It would be too daring to suggest that Le Corbusier had researched Amalarius of Metz, the bishop of Trier and a colleague of Charlemagne, but they shared the same sensibility. The bishop wrote, 'Gazing from afar, behold, I have seen approach the power of God.' And I'm certain that's what Le Corbusier thought at Le Thoronet.

Great architecture speaks to you, although some effort may be required to appreciate what it is saying. Still, one definition of excellence I have personally found to be reliable is that a building is good if it spontaneously improves your mood.

Louis Kahn, a contemporary of Le Corbusier and designer of, for example, the Salk Institute in La Jolla and the India Institute of Management in Ahmedabad, said you must let the bricks talk. This is true. But you need to be prepared to listen. The Three Sisters made Corb want to hear the stone speak quietly, but insistently, above the birdsong and cicadas of the Var.

The idea of going to church with the supposed technocrat Le Corbusier may seem incongruous, but his building designs are suffused with an intense spirituality. As indeed he was . . . despite himself.

'How nice it would be to die swimming toward the sun.'

Le Corbusier, who swam to his death in 1965 from Eileen Gray's villa in Roquebrune

Sex

Gleefully cultivated lust

Beauty has its relationship to sex and time.

To many, beauty may be unbearable because it is – so far from being a joy for ever – fragile and evanescent. Like sex.

Beauty is time's mistress, and time can be an abusive partner. It offers a tantalising glimpse of the eternally valuable ... only to betray us as it corrodes. And the always turning tides of taste make certainty look like a phantasm.

Here the flow becomes interrupted with the question of mortality.

I set myself an imaginative exercise: a lunch with Picasso near his ninetieth birthday. I say this because *timor mortis conturbat me* (the fear of death disturbs me), a refrain from the fifteenth-century Scottish poet William Dunbar's *Lament for the Makers*.

Picasso seemed to have no fear of death, so very, very vigorous was his appetite for life. So here he is, barrel-chested in a striped Breton *pul marin*, deeply tanned, wearing baggy shorts and a battered straw hat.

We are at the Café des Arcades in Biot, near his studio in Vallauris. His chauffeur has just dropped him off in the artist's magnificent Facel-Vega HK500, a deluxe barge mixing the aesthetics of Detroit with the style of Emil Ruhlmann.

Picasso Q&A

Q. Are you a genius or a charlatan?

A. Yes.

Q. Are there limits to human potential?

A. No.

Q. Is imagination valuable?

A. Of course. Because if you can imagine something, it is already real.

Q. Why do you experiment continuously?

A. I do things I cannot do so I can learn how to do them.

Q. What is your greatest achievement?

A. Seduction. And my work is the ultimate one.

Q. What are you looking for?

A. I don't seek, I find.

One of Picasso's last major works was a suite of twenty-five etchings made in 1968; each shows the painter Raphael cavorting in a splendidly uninhibited style with his mistress La Fornarina, the Baker's Daughter. An admiring Pope Julius II looks on.

As if to demonstrate that, for Picasso, making art and making love were not to be separated, in the etchings Raphael does not trouble to put down his brushes, no matter how gymnastic a coupling position he adopts with the Baker's Daughter.

Picasso was working until just a few hours before he died on 8 April 1973. But his last self-portrait was a year before, a crayon piece described as 'Self-Portrait Facing Death'.

The ancients identified the relationship between sex and death as a competition between Eros and Thanatos. One reason the Old Masters have so much more resonance than the Moderns is that there is almost always an intimation of mortality. And Picasso ranks in stature with the Old Masters.

Even in, say, a frivolous François Boucher of a pretty naked girl lolling on cushions there is the shadow of something darker than her pink bottom. Perhaps especially that pink bottom. Yet very few have detected intimations of mortality in Koons' $91-million silver bunny, nor has anyone surely ever found his rabbit erotic. Unless, that is, you are someone who finds cash price titillating.

'Rooted in lust and cultivated with glee.'

Peter Schjeldahl on Picasso's erotic art in
The New Yorker (2001)

But when Pierre Daix, a journalist on *Le Quotidien de Paris* and his biographer, visited Picasso, he irreverently held up the harrowing portrait to his face, and smiled, making it very clear that the fear shown in the picture was an artistic conceit. Picasso was still very much alive and busy making etchings of an erect this and a damp that.

It wasn't love or romance that kept him young but . . . sex.

'It takes a hundred times more intelligence to make love than to command an army.'

Ninon de Lenclos, a courtesan of Henri IV and author of
La coquette vengée (*The Flirt Avenged*) (1659)

The Trouble with Taste
How to escape The Chamber of Horrors

Taste is the way we express and enjoy our preferences. People get agitated about taste because it betrays more of the soul – more of your values – than financial net worth or, say, sexual preferences. No one will blame you for being poor. Even if they blame you for being rich. And no one will ever dare blame you for wanting to be bound in latex and chains and urinated upon by a trans woman in a leopard-skin leotard suspended above you in a titanium cage.

But you *will* be judged by your interior design. Or your goods and chattels.

Sitting at dinner next to a hostess I had already found a little demanding, I was asked what I thought of her plates. I demurred, saying, 'Look, I'm having a lovely time. Let's not get into a treacherous area. Let's not have a discussion we will regret.'

But she smiled coyly, fluttered made-up eyelids and said, 'But you must. You must. You're Mr Design Guru, after all.' There was more fluttering.

I repeated my demurral, suggesting several other areas of conversation, including how much she was worth and whether wearing latex had erotic potential. But she insisted on a comment about the plates.

So, I capitulated, saying, 'Well, if you insist. But I have warned you. My honest opinion is that they are cynical middlebrow junk and look as though they were bought from Boots the Chemist. I wouldn't give them house room, and I am surprised you have.'

I smiled thinly. She now banged the table in indignation, stood up and shrieked at her husband, 'Jasper! You have invited this, this, this ... *man* here and he has *insulted* me in my own house!'

Excuses were made, and I left before the M&S *crème brûlée* was served by a shuffling and scowling Filipina.

It was easier in the eighteenth century when there was a single standard of taste and really no disputing about it, one that had been agreed since the Romans said *de gustibus non est disputandum*.

Anyone could achieve 'taste' through a mixture of education and aspiration. You had a Chippendale pattern book for the furniture. The seasons of fashion were very slow. Architecture had its orders. There was no taste for the exotic or for experimentation in food. Every kitchen had its copy of Hannah Glasse, and no woman of the house would be seen near a stewpot or a preserving pan. Curiosity was not considered valuable. Certainty thrived and was not much tested. Every artist from Joshua Reynolds to William Hogarth knew this:

'Fitness of the parts to the design for which every individual thing is formed, either by art or nature, is first to be considered, as it is of great consequence to the beauty of the whole.'

William Hogarth, *Analysis of Beauty* (1753)

But Hogarth had not anticipated the aesthetic chaos which industrialisation and new social classes brought to the nineteenth century.

That there can be variations in taste is a modern innovation.

The best guide to taste I know was compiled in 1909 by a now obscure German-Moravian curator called Gustav Pazaurek, who established a 'Cabinet of Bad Taste' in Stuttgart's craft museum. He was very much in the English didactic tradition of Henry Cole, who had created a notorious 'Chamber of Horrors' which moved to the South Kensington Museum, the forerunner of the V&A, in 1857. The concern here was to illustrate 'False Principles' in design in order to shame manufacturers into improvement by improving popular taste.

Pazaurek knew a thing or two about false principles and determined that there were five categories of errors that could lead to ugliness: Material Mistakes, Design Mistakes, Decorative Mistakes, Kitsch Mistakes and Contemporary Mistakes. Few lists are more mesmerically fascinating. It is too German to reproduce in full, but an edited version – presented almost in poetic form – nonetheless reveals some of the persuasive force of his reasoning. I suggest reading it in a trance-like state. What follows is what is to be avoided.

Inferior materials, knotty wood, poor alloys, toxic substances, cheap processes, concealed flaws, distorted moulds, spotted glaze. Objects made of human or animal parts, including bone, skin, fingernails, rhino horns, ostrich eggs, antlers, teeth, vertebrae, feathers, fish scales, lizards, lobster claws, butterflies and beetles, egg membrane, nuts, spices, ferns, fungus, coloured sand, ice and bread. Painstaking hobbies which overtax materials. Handicrafts which ignore the inherent properties of a material. Anything made of an inappropriately costly material. One material crafted to ape the character of another. Shallow material puns. Surrogate materials pretending to be more valuable ones, or vice versa. Flat patterns made into 3-D objects, or vice versa. Anything made either too heavy or too light. Anything with sharp edges; a vessel which does not pour; a handle uncomfortable to hold; anything which cannot be cleaned with ease. Combination objects not optimally suitable for either purpose. Functional lies, including architectural ornament. Functional objects in forms that have no intelligent relationship to their purpose. Machine production that apes the effects of handicraft. Frivolous inventions. Forgeries. Obtrusive or odd proportions. Manic ornamentation. Decoration used to disguise flaws. Unskilled or unintelligent use of decoration, such as ignoring the natural logic of a botanical motif. Surface invasions: marbling wood or paper, gilding porcelain or glass. Any decoration created by accident: ink blots, poured glaze, melted wax, pictures drawn in a trance. Originality. Mockery or misuse of national emblems. Anachronisms and exotica. Exaggerated finishes, including iridescence and fluorescence. Primitivism and folk art. Jingoism, souvenirs, folklorica, sportsmen's artefacts, religiosity. Brutalising objects that encourage aggression. Anything made for children. Wasted resources, especially single-use or disposable objects. Pollution. Animal trophies. Sexism and racism. Exaggerated claims of exclusiveness.

A better guide to aesthetic depravity has yet to be written . . .

Pablo Escobar's Taste

In his Hacienda Nápoles near Medellín in Colombia, the *narcotraficante* had South America's largest motocross track, twenty-seven lakes and a zoo stocked with animals donated by street people. When this zoo failed, Escobar contacted a private zoo in Dallas and imported $2-million worth of giraffes, kangaroos and elephants.

. . . although Michael and Jane Stern's 1990 *Encyclopaedia of Bad Taste* brings Pazaurek helpfully up to date with horrors that could not have been imagined in 1909.

Here is an authoritative gloss on contemporary kitsch that, again, makes hilarious reading in itself.

It is difficult to define beauty. It is almost as difficult to define ugliness. But it is easy to identify brainless rubbish.

Aerosol Cheese, Ant Farms, Artificial Grass, Artistry in Denim, Body Building, Breasts (enormous), Candle Art, Cedar Souvenirs, Chihuahuas, Christmas Trees (artificial), Day–Glo,

Dinosaur Parks, Driftwood, Elvisiana, Fake Fur, Feminine
Hygiene Spray, Fingernail Extremism, Fish Sticks, Fuzzy Dice,
Gags and Novelties, Hawaiian shirts, Hellenic Diners, Jogging
Suits, Las Vegas, Lawn Ornaments, Leisure Suits, Leopard Skin,
Liberace, Limousines, Loud Ties, Macramé, Malls, Maraschino
Cherries, Meat Snack Foods, Miniature Golf, Mobile Homes,
Nehru Jackets, Nodding-head Dolls, Novelty Wrestling,
Pantyhose Crafts, Dolly Parton (see above), Pepper Mills (huge),
Pet Clothing, Polyester, Polynesian Foods, Poodles, Reclining
Chairs, Shag Rugs, Snow Globes, Spam, Surf 'n' Turf, Tattoos,
Taxidermy, Troll Dolls, Tupperware, Unicorns and Rainbows,
Velvet Paintings, Wax Museums, and White Lipstick.

**The problem with mediocrity is that it recognises no
condition higher than its own.**

Charming
Nice versus nasty

'The luxury of a false religion is to be unhappy.'

Sidney Smith, from Saba, Lady Holland,
A Memoir of the Reverend Sidney Smith (1855)

Here's an unarguable truth: no one has ever said, 'I wish I were less charming.'

Charm is free and priceless. Its generosity makes people happy. No one loves a misery. Why not acclaim the world and the people in it?

One reliable way to extract maximum value from existence is to treat every meeting with any person at any time as an infinitely precious experience which, if managed with style and good humour, can be richly productive of positive feelings for all concerned. If life's a stage, you can be the impresario, the playwright and the lead actor. You can also collect the ticket money.

Evolutionary psychologists know that friendships are not only life-enhancing, but also life-extending.

Meeting someone is an opportunity to perform. Or, as novelist Jay McInerny put it with not a small amount of brittle Manhattan cynicism, it's a good idea to treat every person you meet as if you have just been given secret information that they will soon become astonishingly rich.

Leventeia

This is a quality much admired by Patrick Leigh Fermor, who was himself memorably described by a schoolmaster as 'a dangerous mixture of sophistication and recklessness'. PLF discovered *leventeia* when travelling through Greece and fighting with partisans. It 'embraces a range of characteristics: youth, health, nerve, high spirits, humour, quickness of mind and action, skill with weapons, the knack of pleasing girls, love for singing and drinking, generosity . . . a universal zest for life, the love of living dangerously and a readiness for anything.'

Why not turn every social encounter into a work of art and a seduction? Why not make every single meeting an educated and elegant game? It may be better, Raymond Loewy once observed, to be envied than pitied, but it is surely better to be liked than disliked.

And while charm can make sceptics suspicious and cynics envious, it is really rather difficult actually to hate someone for being charming.

What Is Charm?

'Artfulness enchanted with a dash of self-mockery.'

Duncan Fallowell (private correspondence)

To comment on charm is itself a charming gesture. The person who calls you charming is trying to charm you. And in this mutually enriching reflexiveness, this well-mannered rally of delicate goodwill and fine gestures, lies the fascination inherent in one of the most sophisticated weapons in our battle for attention. If I am charming, I will win. And even if I do not win, I will have lost with style and grace.

Charm is a powerful weapon that is also mysterious, romantic and appealing. It is a subtle, but irresistible, commodity. It beguiles, then overwhelms, but never overwhelms immediately. Like great paintings, it only reveals itself slowly. And, continuing its interesting complexities, charm is as difficult to define in substance as it is easy to detect in effect.

We know, or soon learn, that charm is a reliably efficient negotiating tool in love or in business. It's a warm and glowing attribute, a winning characteristic. The charmer feels good about himself and makes others want to share that feeling – to make them feel good about themselves. Charm is a multiplier of good feelings. It is a lubricant, a fuel, a salve. Charm will give you a presence that others find attractive.

Additionally, and very likely, charm will also deliver a slight, but insistent, whiff of erotic possibilities. With charm, you can create good situations and extract yourself from bad ones. With charm, you will inspire the envy of men and the interest of women. Or, at least, most of them most of the time. No one hates a charmer, but, then again, not everyone admires him.

Charm can be confused with flattery. In *The Inferno*, Dante has pimps and seducers standing in a ditch where they are distressingly flagellated by horned demons. Pimps and seducers deserve punishment. But so too do flatterers, many of whose characteristics may also belong to the pimp and to the seducer.

So low is Dante's opinion of flatterers that he puts them in the ditch next door, adjacent to the harlot Thaïs, who is, like the pimps and seducers, awash with sewage. Excrement is a significant motif here. Beatrice, observing the scene, says, 'These wretched souls stewed in human filth suffer for the crime of flattery.' The river of filth in which they stew is a symbol of the flattering garbage they have spoken.

Like everything to do with manners, charm can only be understood in context. It is a social weapon which you can aim at specific targets: you cannot be charming to yourself.

People can be victims of charm as readily as they can be its beneficiaries. To experience someone's charm is not always to enjoy benefits. People can fall under charm's spell – and spells, as all shamans and magicians know, can be bad as well as good.

The Charmer and the Psychopath

At this point it needs to be said that the exercise of charm has something in common with the manipulative stratagems of the psychopath. You can find a good working definition of this catastrophic condition in Hervey M. Checkley's 1941 classic of psychiatry *The Mask of Sanity*. The motif of the mask immediately suggests disguise and dissimulation in its primary subject matter: the conduct of a good life and its contrast with an aberrant psyche.

Checkley's description of the psychopath might, with small modifications, serve in some respects as a description of the charmer. The psychopath is someone at once intelligent, unreliable, dishonest, irresponsible, self-centred, shallow and lacking in empathy. The variance is only at the end: charmers have empathy, but in other respects it's a good checklist.

Like the charmer, the psychopath has a method. And each may be, at different parts of the conquest process, persuasive and attractive too. The method has three phases: assessment, manipulation and abandonment. With the psychopath, cruelty and criminal activity are the end result. The charmer is less damaging, since the victim will feel no hurt greater than that of a temporary seduction, but the process is similar.

First, the charmer finds his victim, either a target of opportunity at a cocktail party or a premeditated one in a business plan. Second, with witty and engaging exchanges, he then exercises his charm in order to achieve his romantic or his professional goals. Third, he then moves on to his next target and the cycle recurs. Recurrence is an important idea here, since people with charm are always restless in wanting to give it exercise. Charm is not idle. It is, and this sounds paradoxical, psychologically aggressive. This is surely an element in the definition.

What exactly is meant by calling a man charming? He has curiosity without being intrusively inquisitive. He has a confident, but not swaggering, bearing that's modified by a sensitive and intelligent reticence in the way he holds himself. He does not sulk, nor does he strut. It's a matter of balance, and he finds a physical posture in between. He engages. He listens. He is empathetic. He knows the value of a pause.

The charming man is also well dressed, but this dress sense is not ostentatious and probably owes not very much to fashion. There's a lightness and judgement to it all. It should, they used to say, take ten minutes before you realise someone is well dressed. It might take as long to realise you are being charmed.

You would never really argue with a truly charming man, because a part of charm's purpose is to disarm attacks. In the event of a disagreement, you'd find yourself being gently manipulated. But you'd feel neither bitterness nor regret about this manipulation. On the contrary, you'd probably feel grateful. In fact, you'd feel as if you'd been in touch with a higher sort of being.

The word 'charm' does not actually appear in Baldassare Castiglione's *Courtier*, but this 1527 bestseller became perhaps the single greatest influence on our idea of the English gentleman and his charming ways.

It was one of the first self-help books; in fact, one of the very first popular printed books in any genre. The book was produced by the Venetian Aldus Manutius, almost the first publisher in our modern sense. So, it is amusing to note that, as a literary category, self-help has finer cultural and longer historical credentials than biography or literary fiction.

Curiously, despite the nation's fascination with manners, good comportment and *bella figura*, modern Italian does not have a word for charm (perhaps because Castiglione was less influential in his native land than he was in England). The closest an Italian can get to the English notion is to say *simpatico* (literally 'sympathetic'), but that's a term which carries a lot less meaning. It may well be a very good thing to be *simpatico,* but it is more a passively observed characteristic than an actively managed manipulative stratagem.

Castiglione himself was described as **'indecisive, fussy, snobbish and ambitious'.** But his courtier was made of finer stuff: he must be extremely refined (with all the artifice that word suggests). The smooth polish of surface effects is the courtier's aim. That's the way charm works.

Charm demands an audience, as do feats of bravery. You can't be charming to yourself.

Castiglione says that the ambitious courtier should bear in mind that 'if he fights well in battle, he must make sure his commander sees him do so'. At the same time, it is not gentlemanly to hurry anything. The gentleman must have the accomplishments of knowledge and the capacity to move at speed . . . but these must be *disguised*.

Crucially, the gentleman must always actually be more than he appears to be. But the gentleman–courtier is certainly not without his vanity, even if he makes it his business to suppress obvious self-interest. Charm offers camouflage in the battle for attention.

And while the good courtier must be refined, well presented, courteous and brave, as well as a sparkling conversationalist, none of these should dominate his personality. It was always a matter of balance. In the same way, a modern charmer would fail were he too harsh or insistent. Balance is everything.

With this right balance achieved, the result would be an overall effect which Castiglione called *sprezzatura*. It is untranslatable, as it should be, but the *Oxford English Dictionary* defines it as 'studied carelessness'.

Charm engages and delights, even as it deceives and evades. But if a balance of engagement and delight remains after the deceptions and evasions have long been forgotten, then charm is one of the most valuable attributes a person can possess.

It is the ability, as Albert Camus put it, of getting someone to say 'yes' without them realising they have been asked a question.

Luxurious Allsorts
All the superfluities and none of the necessities

Any fool can lead a busy and expensive life. Today's authentic luxuries are private contemplation, empty space and absolute silence.

'Luxury' is an evocative and difficult word. And, in some quarters, it has become a global Esperanto for certain expectations of what the world should be.

Luxury is always a questionable idea, tragically staining, I believe, everything it touches. But Coco Chanel believed something more witty. Luxury, she said, is not the opposite of poverty. It's the opposite of vulgarity. Her notion of luxury was founded in an austere aesthetic acquired from the nuns who taught her.

Almost every sense of the word recorded in the *Oxford English Dictionary* is a negative one: lasciviousness, lechery, indulgence, shamelessness. It describes an inclination towards the costly.

It has its historic basis in the degenerate Roman emperors so gleefully described by Edward Gibbon in *The Decline and Fall* and the Renaissance popes so colourfully described by

Frederick Rolfe in his magnificently odd *History of the Borgias* of 1901. Then there was the bling of 'Le Gout Rothschild' and the *nouveaux riches* who followed them. 'No matter how modest,' a Rothschild once grandly declared, 'no garden should have fewer than five acres of woodland.'

'Luxury at present can only be enjoyed by the ignorant; the cruellest man living could not sit at his feast unless he sat blindfolded.'

John Ruskin, *Unto This Last* (1860–62)

The word has always had a troubled history.

Etymologically, it is from the Latin '*luxus*', meaning abundance. (So, when Toyota wanted to create a luxury brand combining senses of Rex, for regality, with sumptuous privilege, it coined the marvellous Japlish 'Lexus'.)

In the seventeenth century, 'luxuriance' meant 'habitual use of what is choice or costly', something I think we might all recognise. Notions of exquisiteness and indulgence were soon added to the meaning. By the late eighteenth century, these were complemented by disturbing ideas of decay and corruption, the ones noted by Gibbon.

Luxury is always perplexing. While the Utilitarian philosopher Jeremy Bentham insisted that 'necessaries come always before luxuries', the architect Frank Lloyd Wright said he didn't give a damn about life's necessities, provided he had an ample supply of life's superfluities.

In that luxury involves privilege and pleasure, it's a human fundamental, an appetite we all possess. At a certain stage of cultural development, there's a need for standout: to signify promotion above mere mortals. The Roman *vir triumphalis* wore a purple-and-gold toga, a laurel crown with red boots, and sported a garishly painted face as he was drawn magnificently through the city.

We can track our crisis by tracking concepts of 'luxury'.

But ever since circa 1959 when Ford decided a version of its robustly plebeian Anglia was 'deluxe', simply because it had a heater and a chrome surround to the radiator grille, concepts of luxury have become treacherous territory for the fastidious.

Sixty years after the Ford Anglia Deluxe, you can buy a luxury lavatory cleaner.

Gibbon on Luxury

'Under the Roman Empire, the labour of an industrious and ingenious people was variously, but incessantly, employed in the service of the rich. In their dress, their table, their houses, and their furniture, the favourites of fortune united every refinement of convenience, of elegance, and of splendour, whatever could soothe their pride, or gratify their sensuality. Such refinements, under the odious name of luxury, have been severely arraigned by the moralists of every age; and it might perhaps be more conducive to the virtue, as well as happiness, of mankind, if all possessed the necessaries, and none the superfluities of life.'

Edward Gibbon, *The Decline and Fall of Roman Empire* (1776)

Any discussion of luxury, whose values shift continuously, ends up being a description of the contest between modesty and excess. Of not quite enough being in contest with rather too much.

It's traditional advice on good manners to leave the party with them all wanting more. But Andy Warhol's motto was 'Always leave them wanting less'. This was advice followed by the Shah of Iran when he, we now can see *hubristically*, decided to celebrate two and a half millennia of Persian monarchy. The celebration, held in October 1971, was one of the most luxurious, and sinister, events of recent years. I don't know whether ayatollahs have a concept of *hubris* . . .

The Shah bought 250 red Mercedes-Benz limos to ferry guests. There was catering by Maxim's of Paris, staff wore Lanvin uniforms, linen was by Porthault and everyone drank vintage Dom Perignon. This in the desert near Isfahan! So incongruous, vulgar and aggressive was the display of ostentatious wealth that the young (future Ayatollah) Khomeini condemned it as the 'Devil's Festival'. Luxury, therefore, had some role in stimulating Islamo-fascism.

Excess always occurs where new wealth is found. Artisans from the monastery at Sergiyev Posad worked on the gold trim in the cabin of *Vir Triumphalis*, Vladimir Putin's personal Ilyushin Il-96 300-PU, one of the fifty-eight aircraft in his fleet. London newspapers reported that a Middle Eastern client recently rented a whole suite at a West End hotel to accommodate the bulging shopping bags acquired during a fitful orgy of consumption.

Meanwhile, recent US research says people are unhappy when they earn more than $60,000 per annum. But there is a stubborn resistance from old-school spenders: *Forbes* magazine publishes a Cost of Living Extremely Well Index (CLEWI), a source of rich, if unintentional, comedy. *Forbes*'s basket of ultraluxe goods includes an ebonised Steinway Model D Concert Grand, a Hatteras 75 yacht, a Rolls-Royce Phantom, a pair of Purdey guns, one kilogram of Petrossian Oscietra caviar, Purity Doppio Ajour linen sheets, a Learjet 70 and a Hermès Clemence Jypsiere *sac à main*.

The more sophisticated you are, the more likely you will prefer simplicity . . . even austerity. **'Happiness,' John Stuart Mill believed, 'comes from limiting desires, rather than trying to satisfy them.'**

Coco Chanel always deserves the penultimate, mysterious word: 'Luxury is a necessity that begins where necessity ends.' Or as Manolo Blahnik, celebrity cobbler, puts it, 'The greatest luxury is being free.' Free, that is, from the pink YSL studded goat-hair ankle boots and the ebonised Steinway grand piano.

An Abundance of Simplicity
Less is more than you think

S implicity is actually more satisfying than complexity ... and more difficult to achieve.

Can you ever have too much simplicity? Strange to say, but simplicity in art and design is the end result of some rather complicated processes.

'Minimalism is actually complex and layered and can only be appreciated by a tutored intellect: anyone not aware of the history of art would look at a Minimalist interior and think: "Poor lambs, they can't afford furniture and carpet."'

Sydney Staines (in conversation)

Victorian thought was a mess of different ideas and beliefs, of industry and science competing with religion and art for the attention of the public. Should the new Foreign Office be designed to look like a Roman Renaissance palazzo or a Flemish town hall? Who knew?

Post-postmodern thought, the place we are by my esti-
mation right now, is a turgid mess of cultural relativism and
identity politics when any declaration of excellence or preference is howled down or called out as elitist by a braying mob
which seems to think everything is as good as everything else.

In between Victoriana and our perplexed condition came
modernism, a flawed belief system for sure, but one which
gave the nod to the value of simplicity. Modernism is really all
about wanting to tidy things up.

Thoughts on Simplicity

There has been a functionalist strain in European thought since
Plato, but twentieth-century German designers raised it to a
state of polemical art.

Peter Behrens designed everything for AEG, the mighty
German electrical-engineering concern, from buildings through
appliances to posters. He believed that 'we have no alternative
but to make the world more simple, less complicated'.

Henrich Tessenow built influential social housing. He said,
'The best is always simple, but the simple is not always best.'

Dieter Rams was the designer of Braun electrical goods
who created first the white box and then the black box. His
work fed straight into Apple's influential designs. Rams said,
'Quiet is better than loud, unobtrusive is better than exciting, small is better than large, light is better than heavy, plain
is better than coloured, harmony is better than divergency
. . . neutral is better than aggressive.'

Indeed, simplicity of one sort or another was at the core of
High Modernist theology. That simplicity might be a painting
with no content, a 'concrete' poem with neither punctuation

nor capitalisation or a chair made of tubular steel, inspired by a bicycle's handlebars.

Of course, there really is nothing at all simple about any of these. But what they share is, at least by the lights of, say, Piet Mondrian, e e cummings or Mart Stam, an ambition to shuffle off the clutter of past associations and make something *new*.

'Voluntary Simplicity' was a term adopted by sociologists Arnold Mitchell and Duane Elgin in 1977 to describe the educated response to the unmanageable scale and complexity of the new global institutions becoming alarmingly apparent in the later twentieth century.

A Shopkeeper on Simplicity

'I think the important things are contentment, easy living and simple, elegant qualities – certainly not flaunting extravagance by using expensive, overworked materials. Value lies in intelligent design, beautiful materials and thoughtful manufacture. Products that are hugely expensive and designed to proclaim wealth are correctly described as "bling" and announce vulgarity, insensitivity and stupidity. Certainly, seamless service is an important element of relaxed luxury – expensive, but worth every penny, and a great contributor to easy, contented living. As William Morris said, have nothing in your home that you do not consider beautiful or useful or relevant to contemporary life. This principle is still ignored by the nouveau riche who seem to want to boast visually about their success and wealth. An egg is plain and beautiful. A Fabergé Egg suitable only for oligarchs. Good service is the ultimate component of contentment. By service I mean people who do things you don't want to do yourself. A perfect, serene and sensitive housekeeper, a cook, a cleaner, a gardener, a chauffeur, a secretary . . . all diligent, hard-working and honest. As the billionaire Nubar Gulbenkian said when asked about his perfect meal and companion: "Just me and a damned good head-waiter." Meanwhile, a magnum makes even *vin ordinaire* a luxury.'

Terence Conran (private correspondence)

Simplicity is hard won, but so too is its close relation: privacy.

Our notion of privacy is an invention of recent history, not much older than the electric telegraph. Privacy is about personal identity, sex, hygiene, manners, architectural space, human rights, religious contemplation and creative solitude.

Privacy was one of the modern world's best inventions and one of the post-postmodern world's worst casualties. The valuable pleasures of privacy are in danger of being lost to a public orgy of connectivity. We are threatened by personal space-invaders: predatory Big Data are colonising private life. The reason Google wants to develop a self-driving car is to acquire an acquiescent captive audience whose attention it can sell to its advertisers. Forget Tech. Google is an advertising agency and as cynical and amoral as every other of its kind.

But before The Great Isolation, a new taste for privacy was already developing amongst the affluent. The John Lewis department store will sell you a 'rotating summerhouse', with a capacity of ten passengers bent on communal recreation or working from home. It is £19,000. Princeton University Press's boom in A-frame houses was a surprise success: it addressed a primal urge amongst the sophisticated to rediscover the primitive hut. The literature for all these huts, pods and cabins tends to mention, in rapturous tones, spruce, birch and cedar ... as opposed to resin-bonded aggregate or COR-TEN steel.

Infatuation with the cabin has its source in an eighteenth-century book, perhaps more often quoted than read. This is Marc-Antoine Laugier's *Essai sur l'Architecture*, which was published in Paris in 1753.

Laugier was a churchman who critiqued the conventions of neoclassicism, with its strict architectural language; instead, he valorises 'the primitive hut'. His suggestion is that the very origins of architecture lie in a prehistoric past when trees were bundled together to form an elementary dwelling.

According to eighteenth century architectural theorists, including the Abbe Laugier, the origins of architecture were in a primitive hut whose structure aped the forest where it stood.

Architecture, in this reading, emerges from the benign anarchy of nature, not from the imposition of and response to academic rules. It is about shelter, not status. And Laugier takes his place alongside Jean-Jacques Rousseau as an example of how, in the brightly lit scientific Enlightenment, there was in Francophone culture an undertow towards the primitive. Laugier's 'Primitive Hut' is perhaps where Rousseau's 'Noble Savage' lived.

This hut has been called 'Adam's House in Paradise'. Nice to think of David Cameron choosing a retro-kitsch shepherd's wagon as a secluded place to write his memoirs: in a crisis, the allure of rough primitive values touches even the most smooth and worldly of ex-prime ministers.

Only rarely is advanced technology involved in the new cabin culture, but you can buy a 'Seedpod', which I think is manufactured of engineered plastic and, like the escape capsule in a B-52 bomber, allows you sanctuary from a harsh environment. And, yes, there *is* an explicit religious suggestion in the word 'sanctuary'.

A surprise publishing hit of 2015 was a book called *Cabin Porn* by Steven Leckart and Zach Kleinis. This began as a help-ful-hints blog from a fifty-five acre commune in upstate New York. And it is surely significant that Kleinis made his money from Vimeo, a popular hosting website responsible for a lot of digital noise. So, here's a poacher turned gamekeeper.

The cabin craze has evolved into the van craze. In the US, the market for expensively fitted-out vans exploded. Circa 2020, vans with sleeping quarters added a very American notion of mobility to the static hut. These were not mere panel vans with a plywood-and-foam bed, but mobile hotel suites with rainwater showers and clever HVAC (heating, ventilation, air-con) and technologically sophisticated Japanese lavatories which blow warm air to parts the sun never sees. Leland Gilmore of Benchmark Vehicles, a supplier of such things, told the *New York Times*, 'These are little escape vessels, escape pods.' (Interestingly, as a footnote in the history of taste, observers noticed a distinct cultural divide between these new-generation deluxe vans, often imported Mercedes-Benz Sprinters, and the older generation made-in-USA Winnebago Recreational Vehicles (RVs), the former being middle class and Democratic, the latter being redneck and Republican.)

If anyone doubts the value of privacy, consider the bolt on the lavatory door: contemplate it and its various mean-ings. Here is a device with power and authority, one whose own apparent simplicity carries a fair weight of meaning. It is a social on-off switch, a satisfying mechanical demonstration of how pleasing senses of seclusion and security might be achieved by simply sliding a bolt.

But this is something relatively new in civilised life. In the Middle Ages, the *toilette* was a communal, even social activity. A woman would get dressed and groomed in the company of servants. Complete nakedness was perhaps not commonplace (indeed, if woodcuts are any indication, many medieval folk went to bed and made love fully clothed). But our notion of intimacy, of things best seen and done in private, would not have been understood.

As late as 1676, the Marquise de Sevigny, seventeenth-century France's greatest letter writer, paid a visit to the Duchesse de Bourbon and found her using curling tongs and a powder puff while, at the same time, dipping her bread in a bowl of *bouillon* during lunch. What we now see as essentially private was once a social spectacle. The Duchesse's servants would have watched as she used the bidet.

The rationalists of the eighteenth century found this palaver ludicrous. Rousseau, taking time off from his Noble Savage, asked 'Without the dressing-table, what could one do with life from noon to nine?'

But later in the eighteenth century, as mains water became a possibility, these functions began to decouple themselves from the public gaze, and the rituals of the *toilette* were removed, first, to a semi-private alcove protected by a modesty curtain.

Soon, this began to appear on architectural plans as a separate room, and the public rituals of the *toilette* now became the private experience of going to the toilet. And the value of this privacy was emphasised by that bolt on the door.

Of course, that privacy is threatened if your smartphone comes with you to the loo. And pay attention to that bolt.

This is not the first time that a crisis in public health has excited a taste for privacy and seclusion. During the Great Mortality of the fourteenth century, when the Black Death ravaged England, religious recluses flourished. Known as anchorites, they sourced their taste for seclusion and exclusion in the masochistic practices of early Christians in the Holy Land. Their inspiration was the fourth-century Syrian ascetic Simon Stylites, who, in search of religious revelation, chose to spend thirty-seven years sitting on a platform supported on a long pole. Locked up rather than locked down.

The culture of the anchorites was framed in terms of pandemic. While we sheltered in place with Netflix and take-away, anchorites were less comfortably accommodated when avoiding the Black Death. And these severe recluses were alto-gether more constrained and disciplined than mere hermits. A hermit was essentially free but chose his lonely vocation, while anchorites were, normally, bound to a cell attached to a church and were not allowed to leave: their vows of solitude could not be reversed.

Chillingly, the initiation rite was the Office of the Dead, and for company they may have had no more than a pet cat and a chamber pot. Food was passed to them through a window. The chamber pot was, one imagines, solemnly passed back.

But it would be misleading to suggest that an anchorite's seclusion was misery. Very likely, Julian of Norwich (whose manuscript *Revelations of Divine Love* is perhaps the first book by an English woman) volunteered for solitude as a safe quarantine from the Black Death; her austere cell may have had, relative to what was happening in Norwich itself, a certain level of comfort.

Certainly, anyone who has visited one of the grand monasteries of the late Middle Ages – the Certosa di Pavia, for example, just outside Milan – knows from the beautifully decorated cells, the gorgeous gardens, the sonorous plainchant, the impressive refectory and the generous provision of wine from the vast cellars that, while it is true these monks were escaping the world, the world they were escaping was one of dirt, violence and disease. The monk, denied only heterosexual gratification (and not always denied that since there are many accounts of lascivious nuns), led a life of luxury.

Solitude is privacy taken to a higher level. And it is not to be confused with loneliness, any more than privacy is to be confused with privation.

Thoreau's Hut
Solitude: the school of genius

The great authority on the value of solitude was Henry David Thoreau, who has been described as a Yankee saint, a New England Mahatma Gandhi. His first book was in the emerging travel genre. But 1849's *A Week on the Concord and Merrimack Rivers* did not sell well. Most of the original run of one thousand copies was dumped by the printer, and the author bought the lot. Resignedly, he said, 'I now have a library of nearly nine hundred books, over seven hundred of which I wrote myself.'

It was the attitudes of the great religions that interested Thoreau, not their precise doctrine. A 'Harvard Man', he knew about atomists, pneumatologists, atheists, theists, Platonists, Aristotelians, Leucippus, Democritus, Pythagoras and Confucius.

'Each takes us,' he wrote in *Concord and Merrimack*, 'up into serene heavens, whither the smallest bubble rises as surely as the largest, and paints earth and sky for us.'

But then Thoreau went on a different sort of travel adventure: an internal one.

Solitude: A Reading List

Anthony Storr *The Schools of Genius* (1988)

Henry David Thoreau *Walden: Or Life in the Woods* (1854)

Gabriel García Márquez *One Hundred Years of Solitude* (1967)

Daniel Defoe *Robinson Crusoe* (1719)

Walter Raleigh *A History of the World* (1614), written during imprisonment in the Tower of London.

The Divine Comedy (1320) and *Don Quix*ote published (Part 1) 1605; (Part 2) 1615 of Dante and Cervantes were also inspired by their time in prison or in exile.

On 4 July 1845, Thoreau moved into a hut at Walden Pond, Massachusetts, and stayed for just over two years. Here, he was able to maintain a social distance of 1.5 miles from the town of Concord, whither he would amble to buy his necessities. And it must be admitted he was also not far from his mother's house. To be sure, it was no life of privation, and Thoreau's isolation was not in a life-threatening wilderness but in a genteel suburb. And he would often stroll into town for dinner, although the task he had set himself in the woods was to 'learn what are the gross necessities of life'.

Yet in his book *Walden: Or Life in the Woods*, Thoreau distilled his every thought on the disciplines of solitude and the great value to be achieved from the practise of them. **It is often pointed out that *Walden* is more revered than read – its first chapter is a forbidding eighty pages long – but that is just to put him in the same category as, say,**

Cervantes, Dickens and Proust. It is also often pointed out that Thoreau was no ideal citizen, rather a hyper-controlling narcissist wholly lacking in empathy or generosity. But who wrote the rule that great artists must be nice people?

Explaining that he chose to escape 'the noise of my contemporaries' (he had little time for the petty ways of the masses), Thoreau's *Walden* became a counter-culture classic whose most famous line is 'the majority of men lead lives of quiet desperation'. And in Thoreau, Seneca's conceit about calculating wealth by what you can do without surfaced again.

'Simplify, simplify,' he would say to himself. He observed nature. He became self-sufficient, an activity he described as 'making the earth say beans instead of grass'.

He had his books which must 'be read as deliberately and reservedly as they were written'. Indeed, a whole chapter is devoted to 'Reading'. He had three chairs, because there were occasional visitors: he was not an anchorite like Julian of Norwich or Wulfric of Haslebury. Instead, Thoreau of Walden found that the value of the world could be best appreciated by, at least for a moment, stepping aside from it.

Henry James said of Thoreau that he was 'worse than provincial – he was parochial'. But James was a virulent snob who was always chewing more than he had bitten off. And he entirely missed the point. Thoreau remains – despite resonant contradictions and accusations of hypocrisy – the most eloquent spokesman for clever self-sufficiency and an inspiringly simple life. He found value in staring and in digging. 'What else is there in life but curiosity?' he wrote.

His parochialism, which the pompous James despised, was a triumphant affirmation of the spirit. And his monument is a cairn of rocks near to the site of his cabin in the woods. Of course, Thoreau did not stay in his cabin for ever: he was dead at only forty-six. And if he were alive today, he would perhaps find that – paradoxically – modern cities offer more opportunities for nourishing solitude than the quiet desperation of the countryside.

Of course, there were absurdities. Thoreau was no secular saint. When he saw a shipwreck on Cape Cod in 1849, he showed no sympathy for the victims but did sympathise with the wind and the rocks. And he found the beauty of the beach enhanced by the presence of corpses.

I suppose this simply means that Thoreau was, above all, an aesthete. Quite correctly, I believe, he called an unnecessary doormat 'the beginnings of evil'. And if he sold the herbs he grew, he would be on the way to the devil (he did not believe in). His biographer Laura Dassow Wallis described his entire life as 'performance art'. That surely understates the original genius who saw perdition in coconut matting.

But Thoreau realised that solitude was a conceptual matter rather than a condition that could be measured in yards.

You Don't Need to Be in the Woods to Find Solitude

'On anyone who desires such queer prizes, New York will bestow the gift of loneliness and the gift of privacy.'

E.B. White, *Here is New York* (1949)

Maybe, but Thoreau is the reference point for our notion that solitude is necessary to creativity. Certainly, after nearly a quarter of a century of the internet, there is no evidence that collective presence in cyberspace can produce worthwhile art. When solitude is forced rather than elective, it can edge into disagreeable loneliness.

And there are those who might fear boredom in solitude. But boredom can itself be a valuable experience.

Boredom Studies
Beauty is on the other side of boredom

L et's hear it for boredom. There's value in it. Boredom is very
  interesting. At least, the deluxe sort is.

There is even a new discipline called Boredom Studies
emerging.

Boredom: A Thankfully Short Reading List
James Danckert and John D. Eastwood *Out of My Skull: The Psychology of Boredom* (2020)
Alberto Moravia *La Noia* (1960)
David Foster Wallace *Pale King* (2011), a posthumous quasi-fictional memoir about daily life in an Internal Revenue Service office

So far from being a negative state of mind, larded with miserable
streaks of lethargy, apathy, self-loathing, hopelessness and misery,
there's a growing body of opinion, both artistic and scientific,
that boredom may be, or can be considered as, a positive stimulus.

'Everyone is a bore to someone. That is unimportant. The thing to avoid is being a bore to oneself.'

Gerald Brenan, *Thoughts in a Dry Season* (1978)

What is boredom?

French *ennui* is not quite the same as boredom. This '*dégoût de la vie*', or distaste for life, has an etymology shared with the word meaning annoying. In teasing out a definition, it's important to distinguish mere irritation (which is a nuisance) from stultifying boredom (which is an all-consuming funk).

It's a feeling of uselessness with a troubling sense of being unable to escape the condition. You are trapped in a bad place where there is no hope of immediate improvement and no prospect of future relief; it's a Hades of futility whence there is no release. A limbo where tastes are dulled and appetites atrophied, but at the same time where we crave something impossible to identify.

'The desire for desires.'

Leo Tolstoy's definition of agony can be found In
Boredom: short story collection (2013)

Boredom inspired Henry Ford's tinkering mechanical genius and gave us the Model T, motorising the world and expanding the hitherto narrow horizons of, first, Midwest farmers, then, next, all the rest of us.

'Driving is boring, but it's what we do. Most of American life is driving somewhere and then driving back wondering why the hell you went.'

John Updike, *Rabbit at Rest* (1990)

Certainly, the frustration of traffic daily refreshes for most of us the sensation of boredom. The feeling of being hopelessly trapped – as you do in a river of hot, coagulated, fume-spewing metal – is one of the defining conditions of being bored. But that also sets your imagination on vectors of escape. Not least, dreaming of fast cars and open roads.

The traditional view is that boredom is a passive, disengaged state. But it has an exciting side: being bored rouses a search for purpose.

Be that as it may, 'bored to death' is a familiar expression, suggesting something complex and frightening about boredom's relationship to extermination. Can we be so bored that the very last flicker of enthusiasm for life expires and we become permanently defunct?

If you are bored, you want to move on. Boredom is thrilling because your listless, glum, bored individual acknowledges the existence of better words . . . if only he could find them.

'Enduring tedium over time in a confined space is what real courage is.'

David Foster Wallace, *The Pale King* (2011)

Vistas and vectors of escape – in space and time – are everywhere in the discussion for boredom. The bored want escape from the prison of now into the freedom of the past or the future.

So, what makes us bored? People certainly, absence of them perhaps less so. Length is a factor. No one, for instance, has ever wished Milton's *Paradise Lost* were any longer.

Cocktail Parties

'A healthy male adult bore consumes each year one and a half times his own weight in other people's patience.'

John Updike, *Assorted Prose* (1965)

Walter Sickert's *Ennui* was painted in 1914. It illustrates the proposition that there is no known cure for an English Sunday afternoon.

Writers, the most solitary of creatures, often toy with boredom because it fascinates and disturbs. The novelist Alberto Moravia used to walk about Rome and, according to his translator William Weaver, would say to anybody he met, '*Mi annoio. Voglio morire*,' (I am bored. I want to die), although Moravia was, by most accounts, a humorous and good-natured soul who meant nothing of the sort. He wasn't bored and didn't want to die.

Moravia's novel *La Noia,* the SUV of boredom literature, was published in 1960. Here Moravia writes:

> The feeling of boredom originates for me in a sense of the absurdity of a reality which is insufficient, or anyhow unable, to convince me of its own effective existence . . . For me, therefore, boredom is not only the inability to escape from myself, but is also the consciousness that theoretically I might be able to disengage myself from it, thanks to a miracle of some sort.

The question of time passing either too fast or too slow always recurs in discussions of boredom. It is elegiac that happy people rush towards death as time whizzes by, while for the sad time seems endless. Evelyn Waugh, for example, thought 'punctuality is the virtue of the bored'.

John Cage 'wrote' an extremely boring piece of music called *4'33"*, which refers to the precisely four minutes and thirty-three seconds you listen to the absolute silence which he authored. Cage said, 'If something is boring after two minutes, try it for four. If it is still boring, try it for eight, sixteen, thirty and so on. Eventually, one discovers it is not boring at all, but very interesting.'

Listening to John Cage might be a remedy for our overly busy world, where five hundred hours of video are uploaded to YouTube every minute.

If we have any sense, we might want to cultivate boredom to overcome the noise of so many conflicting signals, the better to concentrate on what's truly valuable. The boredom of the rich, it's been said, is more poignant than the boredom of the poor because it's a sign of spiritual poverty. At least the poor know what they want.

If boredom can be productive, so too can other forms of privation. Here the fabulous Victorian lady travellers provide rich source for consideration and inspiration. You look at a photograph of Kate Marsden *circa* 1890, wrapped in what look like very smelly and uncomfortable furs, on her way to Siberia and you do wonder what exactly she wanted to escape from.

Howling jackals, dread crags, fearsome mountains, struggling in mangrove swamps were routine for our Victorian ladies. Lady Hester Stanhope travelled with a tent five or six feet in diameter. This she converted into a mobile latrine with her favourite chamber pot, since she had noted that the endless plains of Latakia in Syria offered no bushes, trees or any cover for 'any little purpose' as she put it.

When Lady Eastlake travelled to Talinn in 1838, it was so cold her eyebrows grew icicles and the sherry froze, an intolerable privation.

In a storm in the Channel in 1862, Lady Duff Gordon declared, 'I am almost ashamed to like such miseries so much.' Later, Mrs W.W. Baillie recorded in *Days and Nights of Shikar* (1921) that it was 'interesting' to have been mauled by a bear. When Violet Cressy-Marcks suffered a snakebite in South America, she reflected, with stoic calm, 'If I was going to die, it was a fine spot for it.'

'No inconveniences,' Isabella Bird said, 'are legitimate subjects for sympathy which are endured in pursuit of pleasure.'

It was boredom that drove them to these dangerous and fascinating extremes.

Believing in Ghosts
Household gods and how to find them

Charm is connected to magic. This is why we speak of 'magic charms'. My grandmother, a descendant of prosperous East End street traders, used to wear a complicated and very heavy gold bracelet festooned with them. I seem to remember they included an ankh and an Eye of Horus – although I am certain my grandmother had not a clue what most of them were, I am sure she recognised the Eiffel Tower and Bambi.

As a small child, I found it fascinating. I still do, but for different reasons. Nice to think that these industrialised trinkets were descended from the protective amulets used by the Egyptians. However, my grandmother came from Bow, not Thebes or Memphis. She used cockney rhyming slang, not hieroglyphics. Still, I like to think the god Thoth knew his way around Bethnal Green Road.

An unanticipated side effect of the digital age and the decline of organised religion is the return of magical thinking. For example, soon after Diana's 1997 death in a speeding S-Class Mercedes – a very twentieth-century demise, involving the Ritz, *paparazzi* and fast cars – improvised wayside shrines, medieval in character, began to appear around the crash site in Paris' Pont de l'Alma tunnel, rather as they once did on treacherous Alpine passes.

Technology tends to bleed mystery and enchantment from the world. Tech is our new religion, but not an altogether satisfactory one. Religion, in James Frazer's influential definition appearing in his anthropological classic of 1890 *The Golden Bough*, demands that we are submissive to an intolerant God, in our case Zuckerberg.

But magic is different and more empowering: it gives us protection. We can put magic to work for us. Especially if we know how to appease the gods.

First, the household gods, nowadays living in that annoying kitchen drawer also accommodating the never-used MagiMix blades of obscure purpose. These were first recognised by the Romans. Known as *lares*, every well-to-do Roman villa had a *larium* in the *atrium* where respects could be paid to these protective deities.

Ceremonies were held three times a month where the paterfamilias would preside, offering the domestic gods salt, milk and wine. Dad would be surrounded by impressive clouds of incense, the better to perform these rites. Additionally, to make the point about continuity, the *larium* would very likely be decorated with death masks of long-gone ancestors. Perhaps their ghosts were present too. Of course, these household gods made their own distinctive contribution to the idea of *genius loci*, that special character attaching to certain places.

But there are lots of other gods with whom we would be wise to be acquainted. And we could take a lead from the Japanese who are as highly evolved in their awareness of the everyday presence of deities as they are in their reverence for the freshest tuna and their aptitude for precision engineering, plus their faddish tastes for owl cafés, eyelid trainers, tentacle porn and cartoon-animal costumes.

Japanese air stewardesses, for example, have a god dedicated to their protection. She is called Benten, and her portfolio also includes the care of designers. Similarly, another god called Jurojin is tasked with looking after barmen and philosophers. This is entirely understandable, since the better sort of philosopher is indistinguishable from a barman.

Of the myriad deities identified by the Japanese, since 1420 at a ceremony in Fushimi, seven are thought of as especially lucky. And every New Year, the Lucky Seven sail a magic ship carrying treasure from Heaven to Earth. It is not clear in the standard accounts whether passengers on this magic ship are attended by stewardesses.

The aerial treasure includes a very convenient-sounding hat of invisibility, a purse whose contents are inexhaustible, a robe of fairy feathers which confers the gift of flight upon the wearer and a splendid magic mallet which when used to strike an object turns that object into hard cash.

So far as I am aware, none of this glorious nonsense has been disproved by science.

I think it is very valuable to believe in ghosts. And I think I have seen one. In the Louvre, there is a 1509 *Portrait of a Young Man* by a middle-ranking Florentine painter called Franciabigio. Not that the sitter is especially handsome, but he *is* interestingly morose and self-possessed. And he looks extraordinarily like me. Or, as a sundial might have said, how I used to look. To short circuit five hundred years is a haunting experience.

But my ghosts are not the ludicrous poltergeists of folklore, the ones who hurl lithobolic missiles, the crazy flying stones that bothered, for instance, Increase Mather, an early president of Harvard renowned for his excessive austerity and bad humour (plus, I imagine, his intense sexual frustration). My ghosts are something more subtle, recognising the life and energy of objects and places. Ghosts leave their traces. They suggest continuity.

Objects have life. And that means the possibility of death too. Our possessions betray us, whispering stories behind our backs. Do not imagine that food-processing wand is entirely mute. There is, indeed, a ghost in the machine.

Cities too. Any mechanism that acquires even a modest level of complexity develops a personality of sorts. Anyone who has been to Pompeii can attest, once you have edited out the tourist coaches and the gimcrack curio sellers, to the existence of its ghosts.

Take Pompeii's erotic art: just look at the *apodyterium* of the suburban baths with scenes of a *ménage à trois* in the Neronian style with Vespasianic overpainting. This art is actually and metaphorically layered; it possesses an original energy that is not to be lost.

That there is energy in stuff can be misconstrued. Staff at the British Museum have often been disturbed by what they fear may be Egyptian mummies shifting about at night in their vitrines, but what was really happening was that static electricity accumulated from entirely natural causes during the day was causing the mummies' bindings to ripple at night.

When he reached the 'Singing Sands' of the Kumtag desert in what is now north-west China, Marco Polo presumed the creepy windblown noises to be the ghosts of earlier travellers, less successful than himself. In the Alpujarras in southern Spain, it is common knowledge that the higher the village, the greater the number of witches in the area. I see no reason to dispute this.

Ruins are architecture's ghosts: they too suggest continuity. The Eternal City of Rome enjoys that eternity because it has been through so many cycles of destruction and rebuilding with what's known as *spolia:* recycled architectural rubble. Reliefs on the Arch of Titus show Roman legionnaires returning with loot from the First Roman–Jewish War; the Colosseum was built in part from *spolia*. Rome's most famous monument contains rubble from Judaea.

The first painting of a ruin was, perhaps, Maso di Bianco's *St Sylvester and the Dragon* in the Santa Croce, Florence, finished in 1340. A little later in the Renaissance, the famous illustrated *Hypnerotomachia* of 1499 treated ruins as a source of speculation and is often cited as the source for 'ruins, beauty of' becoming a fixed idea in the Romantic conception of the world, or at least in the indexes of books that describe it.

It was the ghosts in the ruins of the Roman Forum that inspired Gibbon to write his magnificent *Decline and Fall* of 1776. The taste for ruins continues but has shapeshifted somewhat.

Ruins were taken up with unsavoury relish by Hitler's architect, Albert Speer. His *Ruinentheorie* argued that buildings should be designed to look good when they have collapsed and decayed. But since Rose Macaulay, we now enjoy a sort of weird approval for ruination. Three years after publication of *The Pleasure of Ruins* in 1953, travelling along Spain's Costa de la Luz, Macaulay became convinced of the existence of ghosts near the Roman ruins at Burgos.

One reason we enjoy ruins is that they suggest there is no such thing as finality in art: the Temple of Jerusalem lives on. The paradox of ruins is that they are, so far from being evidence of the fragility of things, evidence of their endurance.

'The modern viewer of old monuments receives aesthetic satisfaction not from the stasis of preservation, but from the continuous and increasing cycle of change in nature.'

Alois Riegl, a pioneer art historian,
The Modern Cult of Monuments (1903)

And ghosts did not disappear in the supposedly technocratic twentieth century. I sometimes suspect they might have even multiplied, in the same fashion that wayside shrines have done. We may have no M.R. James writing superlatively spooky ghost stories, but it's interesting how many important literary figures from the last century were inclined towards the occult.

Take W.B. Yeats, a founder in 1885 of Dublin's Lodge of the Hermetic Society and five years later in London a member of the Hermetic Order of the Golden Dawn. His fellow members included the dodgy con man and scoundrel Aleister Crowley. Yeats's mystically inclined wife was a medium, and together they experienced spirit possession and practised 'automatic writing', later taken up by the Surrealists in Paris.

Or Arthur Conan Doyle, creator of Sherlock Holmes. Isn't it wonderful that an author whose literary reputation was founded on his hero's brilliant powers of rational forensic analysis was also, in 1920, an apologist for the Cottingley Fairies, a puerile photographic hoax using cardboard cutouts?

This was no passing fad of Doyle's brought about by his personal crisis during the First World War, which claimed his eldest son and only brother. The Sherlock author had begun experiments with mesmerism when a junior doctor in the 1880s. 'There is no death,' he liked to say . . . even before he found out that, oh yes, there was. Additionally, he told *The Times* that there really was not much doubt that the archaeologist Lord Carnarvon died as a result of the Curse of Tutankhamun.

Only the dullest person has not felt the presence of the past and its population, as Gibbon did in the Forum that evening he was inspired to write *The Decline and Fall*. It is not difficult, when the crowds have left the Forum, to replicate Gibbons's haunting. This is not mere sentiment: even the baffling language of astrophysics allows for notions of decay and rebirth. And, of course, the indestructibility of energy.

I am no mystic, but it is surely a most valuable thing to believe, not so much in the reality of rectory hauntings as in the depth and endurance of existence. To believe that there is more to life than hydrocarbons and insurance policies and an Amazon Prime account. To believe that something preceded and something else will follow and that, in any case, everything is continuous and only our feeble human grasp of the Universe wants to make distinctions anyway.

Or put it this way: in relationship to the Universe, we are as bewildered as a dog in a library where a string quartet is playing. The dog can hear the noise and see the books but understands . . . nothing.

During The Great Isolation, when the art galleries were all shut, there was excitable talk about the efficacy of virtual museum visits: high-definition digital images sent to your screen could replace intimate, analogue contact. People said that the Raphael Cartoons, for example, could be displayed in their full glory rather better in very-high-definition video than in the gloom of the Victoria & Albert Museum, where they hang in sombre desuetude, ignored much more than their magnificence deserves.

And these enormous Raphael Cartoons, impossible to grasp in the murky light of an Edwardian gallery, could be enjoyed at home, rather than after a risky trip to South Kensington. It is certainly true that museum conservation protocols prevent us from seeing the Raphael Cartoons – or any other sensitive work of art – in the light conditions for which they were designed. It is also true that the colours have faded so that they are, actually, only a pale representative of what the artist intended.

Wouldn't it be better to have easy access to a technologically enhanced improvement in vivid colour with billion-pixel Google details than struggle to a grim old museum to stand bemused, cricking your neck to admire pallid originals? What's the authentic experience? The unsatisfactory dried-up original or a technologically enhanced sexed-up version of it?

The most-famous, most-quoted and least-well-understood argument about authenticity in art was made by the Frankfurt School thinker Walter Benjamin in a 1935 essay sonorously entitled 'Das Kunstwerk im Zeitalter seiner technischen Reproduzierbarkeit'. This, with the elegance native to the English language, is 'The Work of Art in the Age of Mechanical Reproduction'. Benjamin says an authentic work of art has 'testimony to the history which it has experienced', or that it gets knocked about, fades and cracks. And it has a 'presence in time and space . . . [a] . . . unique existence at the place where it happens to be'.

Benjamin believed in **aura**. Or what you might call an environment of ghosts. Meanings accumulate around old pictures: the indefinable life which separates battered originals from even superlative copies, rather as solid corpses, no matter how masterfully embalmed, are not to be confused with fugitive ghosts.

A surprising enthusiast for ghosts was Jacques Derrida, a leading figure in the Paris School of Intellectual Imposture, the father, so called, of Deconstruction, the godfather of postmodern thought, and the source of many an affected and exasperating footnote.

Intellectual Imposture

Derrida and others were spoofed by a New York University physicist called Alain Sokal, who submitted a paper to an academic journal purporting to be an attempt by postmodern thinkers to debunk science itself as a mythical construction. The idea was to show postmodern thinking as absurdly overreaching and even fraudulent. This was the source of Sokal's book *Impostures Intellectuelles* of 1993. It caused delight among the humanities crowd, especially at the *New York Review of Books*, but the prank misfired because Sokal had chosen an obscure journal that was not peer reviewed. What's more, Derrida's response in *Le Monde* won him many friends because of its patience and dignity.

In his own 1993 book called *The Spectre of Marx*, Derrida coined the term 'hauntology', a reference to ghosts, but also a nice play on words, because 'hauntology' sounds, when pronounced by a Frenchman, like a homophone for 'ontology', the philosophical study of existence itself. I imagine Derrida was trying to make a neologism as memorable as Auguste Comte's 'sociology'. As we now know, he failed, but the presence of ghosts in the loftiest deconstructivist mind is, even if the ghosts are ironic ones, powerful evidence of their existence.

The 'spectre' of Derrida's title is, of course, a synonym for ghost. And he was referring to Marx's infamous 1848 manifesto where he declared 'the spectre of communism is haunting Europe'. Derrida writes that 'ghosts arrive from the past and appear in the present'. But we knew that. What's more interesting is that Marx does continue to haunt us from the grave. And he believed in a cycle of birth and rebirth – 'history,' he wrote, 'repeats itself first as tragedy, secondly as farce'.

Of course, the myth of the perpetual return, or eternal recurrence, has been a fundamental of philosophical thought from the Vedic hymns to Albert Camus.

A Utopian Socialist on the Afterlife

'From the observed process of the generation and growth of the body from a microscopic origin . . . the probability of the pre-existence in a sub-atomic or fourth-dimensional state of the being which is manifested in the body, and therefore the probability of the continuance of that being after the dissolution of the body.'

Edward Carpenter, *The Drama of Love and Death* (1912)

There *is* such a thing as *genius loci*; there are such things as lasting values. The gods are embedded in the everyday world . . . but at the same time distinct from it. Ghosts might exist in the imagination, but, as Picasso knew, what's in the imagination is already real.

Some landscapes are special, places where forces are aligned, where history tugs at your senses, where natural landscape and man-made interventions are in a very pleasing harmony. But everywhere is full of meaning. It is just that in some places the ghosts and the gods are in recession: like the rest of us, they probably prefer the Val d'Orcia to the KwikFit depot on Walworth Road.

But you can read anywhere and anything like a book, if only you know how. Places, buildings and objects have stories to tell . . . if you are prepared to listen. And it is valuable to hear them.

The Common Law of Business Practice
The price of everything and the value of nothing

So where are we with value?

The word is nowadays most familiar in the expression 'brand value'. This is the difference between what something is actually worth and what someone is actually prepared to pay for it. Take Tesla, which has now replaced Coca-Cola as the most successful brand in the world. You can do a simple calculation. Subtract from the market capitalisation of Tesla ($253.38 billion on the day I am writing this during The Great Isolation) the value of its declared assets (which are very much less), and the figure you are left with is the value of Tesla's 'brand'.

But this is a cash value, thus not really so very valuable after all. Nor is it a good measure of value: John Milton was paid a mere £10 for *Paradise Lost*.

The most familiar formulation of price being an imperfect guide to merit is what has become known as the Common Law of Business Practice, and it is often attributed to John Ruskin, whose Biblical rhetoric had dominated first nineteenth-century art criticism and later nineteenth-century thinking about the relationship of art to work.

Like buying the best soap, the Common Law states:

There is hardly anything in the world that someone cannot make a little worse and sell a little cheaper, and the people who consider price alone are that person's *lawful prey*.

But Ruskin scholars dispute the attribution, saying nothing in any published Ruskin material says anything of the sort. It was probably invented by an ambitious journalist. Certainly, when it was taken up as a corporate slogan in the Baskin-Robbins ice-cream parlours, it perhaps lost a little of its lofty credibility. Baskin-Robbins is owned by the giant Dunkin' Brands, a specialist in edible fats.

False Economy: Notes Towards a Definition

Frederick the Great, according to the historian Macaulay, fed his children rotten cabbages, leading to a form of malnutrition.

Cheap shoes.

Industrial mayonnaise.

Saving the £50 connection fee charged by John Lewis and plumbing in the new washing machine yourself, only to flood the house and lead to a ceiling collapse costing many thousands to rectify.

The survival of the Common Law of Business Practice is interesting. Although it has defied scholarly attribution to Ruskin, it remains his most famous dictum. It is his ghost and effortlessly transcends the drudgery of textual analysts become immortal. Marcel Proust agreed and said of Ruskin, 'His thoughts are in some sense lent to him for his life-time. On his death, they return to mankind to instruct it.'

Indeed, at the first meeting of the Labour Party, six years after the great critic's death, more attendees cited Ruskin as an inspiration than they did Karl Marx. Now that's what I call an afterlife. And quite something for a career that began as a Very High Tory.

But Ruskin was, to put it no higher, a rather different character to Marx, although they have enjoyed a similarly influential afterlife. And the afterlife of each has achieved a value beyond academic approval, as Ruskin would have wished. Simply put: John Ruskin was one of the greatest *critics* ever.

What Are Critics For?

'The critic's task is to trace a twisted, looping, stutter-stepping, incomplete path toward the truth, and as such to fight an unending battle against premature and permanent certainty.'

A.O. Scott, *Better Living through Criticism* (2016)

Although he disliked the wrong sort of earthbound travel, Ruskin's mind travelled most effectively on a first-class cerebral journey from robust criticism of art to rhapsodic appreciation of nature to inspirational utopian social theories. And thereafter onto what looks very much like barking madness.

The ghost of Ruskin survives and tells us to look at things very, very closely . . . almost anything can be a source of inspiration, given the right attitude and good sightlines. Ruskin attached equal significance to geological samples and to cathedrals. This ghost (possibly with mutton chops and a frock coat) inspires impressive amounts of reflective thought. Proust acquired from his admiration of Ruskin a 'fetishistic reverence' for books and for thinking as well as for minute observation. Which, of course, led to the creation of one of the modern age's greatest written masterpieces, Proust's vast roman-fleuve, *Á la recherche du temps perdu*, which appeared between 1871 and 1922. The title is a reference to Shakespeare, whose ghost is present on almost every one of Proust's pages.

It is not too puritanical to say that enjoyment can be more valuable if there is a little bit of difficulty involved in the pursuit of it. Pain can lead to pleasure.

Scrutiny can be hard work, as Flaubert realised. In his unfinished posthumous novel *Bouvard et Pécuchet,* published in 1881, the year after his death, the two clerks of the title attempt to assemble all the world's knowledge into a single volume which became known as the *Dictionnaire des idées reçus.* A doomed enterprise, Flaubert was forced to admit that a result of even thinking about the compilation was *'Je doute de tout, même mon doute'* (I doubt everything, even my doubt). But this is encouraging, because genuine faith is always fed and fattened by doubt.

Because the purpose of this book is to increase a capacity for enjoyment, especially when alone, I was tempted to give a nod to Henry Miller and title it 'A Guide to Reading in the Toilet'. But instead, that became just a short chapter. Henry Miller was actually diffident about the benefits of reading in the toilet. But I don't think we should follow him too slavishly.

From Chinese sages to nineteenth-century liberal economists and twentieth-century art critics, the consensus is that the most valuable things in the world are beyond cash. Literally, priceless. Indeed, they are beyond any sort of measurement. Love, desire, charm, taste, beauty and wit can all be created and enjoyed without spending much money.

This is why the book ends with that short diversion about ghosts. I am not advocating a cranky embrace of the paranormal, a tumble with the Woman in White, a tussle with the Headless Man, simply wanting to suggest that the uncertainties of existence make ghosts an entertaining possibility. At the same time, local gods being a reality is a fine antidote to the crass horrors of the Met Gala and a world where Mark Zuckerberg has more power than Julius Caesar once enjoyed.

And on rereading, I now find that ghosts, divinity and its various metaphors have been a recurrent, if unexpected, feature in the writing. I suppose one thing being said here is that it really is a good idea to get on terms with ghosts and the gods, wherever they may be. Including the toilet.

And one other thing. Surely *carpe diem* (seize the day) never had more resonance than now.

If you want to do it, do it today. Whatever it is. Remorse is less damaging than regret. You have remorse about something ill-judged which you have done, but regret occurs when you are reminded of all those things you have fastidiously not done. I mean, thy neighbour's wife might be a source of both remorse and regret. It depends how you played it.

Meanwhile, of course, it's good to deal with the here and now, but it's also good to be curious about the there and then . . . as well as the what might be if only because they add pleasure and meaning to the present moment where we are forever located.

Value

Is it inconsistent to advocate a keen enjoyment of immediate pleasures while at the same time encouraging a belief in ghosts, gods and enduring values? Maybe. But consistency is a puerile temptation.

Better, surely, to have twinges of remorse about unwise actions than to be stupefied by an unmodifiable regret that no action was ever taken. I dare say John Mortimer felt some remorse about overuse of his splendid line 'Tell me, is a fuck out of the question?' But I am certain his regret at never having used it would have been more intense.

On the subject of love, or sex, Casanova is a good guide to the journey along the remorse–regret vector. The great lover, charmer, seducer, traveller and wit began his career with a learned academic thesis about whether the Jews should be allowed to build new synagogues, a lively topic in his native Venice since the city with its substantial Jewish population is probably the source of the word 'ghetto'. As well as Shakespeare's famous merchant.

But Casanova is not remembered for a learned academic thesis, rather for his charmingly scandalous behaviour, his elevation of seduction in its every sense to an art form. His entire life was a work of art. Which is exactly as it should be.

'To cultivate the pleasure of my senses was throughout my life my main preoccupation; I have never had any more important objective.'

Casanova, *Histoire de ma vie* (with a publishing history as complicated as his love life)

That was correct in 1798 when Casanova died ... without either remorse or regret. And cultivating the pleasures of the senses seems even more correct and compelling right now when all our values have been threatened and disturbed by the enlarging prospect of a diseased global catastrophe. Casanova's experience with his crowded diary, busy travel schedule and vigorous polyamory was different to Robinson Crusoe's life of privation and solitude. But each teaches us well about harvesting personal resources the better to enjoy our predicament. The perfumed *boudoir* and desert island were both fertile grounds for the growth of inspiring personalities.

Roger-Viollet/Shutterstock

Casanova's popular reputation is founded in a salacious fascination with his incontinent promiscuity, but he was also a serious aesthete committed to an intellectual understanding of sensory pleasure.

Perhaps a future book might be dedicated to the privileged and suave Venetian fornicator, not to the dour and dispossessed Scottish castaway. But that will be for different times.

Right now, we are closer to Crusoe than Casanova. We are, alas, more in need of methodologies about sweeping the floor or reading in the toilet than of knowing effective formulae for love philtres or the best Scarlatti to be played for the purposes of seduction. But these can come later.

Otherwise, in these strange days, *omnia exeunt in mysterium*. Everything is a mystery. Premature and permanent certainties are a delusion, even if Microsoft thinks it can use surveillance and coding to turn the world into a game. The simple fact that nothing rhymes with the ugly word 'algorithm' makes me very suspicious of it.

The conclusion here is that there is not one. You just need to keep asking questions. Cultivate the senses. And enjoy the mysterious glory of the everyday. Because that is all we have got. And there is huge value in realising it.

Acknowledgements

A reliable route to happiness is to think no farther ahead than lunch or dinner. Or so I have found. Most of the good stuff happens around the table. At least, that's what happened here. This book arose out of a long, rambling lunch with its publisher Andreas Campomar, a lunch which began with Chablis, evolved into a memorable Uruguayan tannat (a grape that helps you live for ever) and ended with some majestic Armagnac which solemnised a conversation that was irreverent, unpredictable and, so far as I recall, on occasions really rather funny, on others surprisingly serious. It was Andreas's bold and stylish idea to capture the colour and sense of that conversation in a book so that others, if not able to join our next lunch, could at least join us in spirit. Therefore, thanks to Andreas.

But it occurs to me now that most of the *research* for this book took place over lunch. Often at Table 32 in Polpo on Beak Street in Soho, but sometimes at The Wolseley, Chelsea Arts Club or Athenaeum, over the years I have argued and joshed with a regular bunch of indulgent friends. If there's a thesis here, I must thank my research assistants. First of all Penny Furniss, an expert in the theory and practice of lunch, who likes to hold her own in male company. Then: John Brown, Stuart Gibbons, John Gordon, Jules Lubbock, Simon May, Andrew Nahum, Justin Marozzi, John Pawson, John Preston and Patrick Uden. If I have forgotten anyone, that's because lunch went on too long.

I must also thank Andreas Campomar's colleagues, Sean Garrehy for the splendid look-at-me cover art, and Jo Wickham for wrestling a wilfully undisciplined set of messages into impressive coherence.

A Note on Sources

This is not a book based on academic research, although I have been there and done that. Long ago.

Instead it's a book of opinion, speculation, memory, invention and projection. If a source was used, I have cited it in the main text since I think footnotes reveal an inability to think economically or write succinctly.

But most of the sources are the very many notebooks where, for nearly thirty years, I have been scribbling quotations and observations. Often, these quotations have been paraphrased and repeated in modified form so often by me that they acquire a life and legitimacy of their own. Or, so I believe.

Of course, the net is an astonishing source to plunder and no-one has yet determined how most efficiently and properly to make references to sources found there. The Q&A with Mark Zuckerberg is, obviously, a fantasy, but his answers are sourced in scraps found in the feast that the net offers us. If you Google Zuckerberg's name, it offers 30,800,000 references. 22,400,000 of them on his tastes in food. Here are rich pickings to select crumbs.

Sometimes, I assume well-known book and song titles have become a part of popular currency and need no explanation. When I write 'We can see clearly now the rain has gone', it's a reference to Johnny Nash's 1972 reggae classic 'I Can See Clearly Now'.

Raymond Loewy and Le Corbusier appear often here and their most famous works are long out of copyright. But I have been quoting, possibly sometimes mis-quoting, from Loewy's *Never Leave Well Enough Alone* of 1951 for a long time. And Le Corbusier's opinions are often so familiar they have become universal. But I do find Peter Serenyi's 1975 anthology *Le Corbusier in Perspective* a useful reminder of the old rascal's prejudices and insights.

Index

Afterword

'Some of these little pieces contradict one another since I am apt to think differently at different times, and indeed am capable of thinking opposite things at the same time, but I have made no attempt to rectify this because my instinct has been to write honestly according to my feelings at the moment rather than to put forward a consistent view.'

Gerald Brenan